Ballet Stories

Ballet Stories

Joan Lawson

MAYFLOWER BOOKS
NEW YORK

Copyright: 1978 by Joan Lawson
All rights reserved under International and Pan American
Copyright Convention. Published in the United States by
Mayflower Books, Inc., New York City 10022.
Originally published in England by Ward Lock Limited,
London, a member of the Pentos Group.

Library of Congress Cataloging in Publication Data

Lawson, Joan
    1. Ballets – Stories, Plots, etc. – Juvenile Literature.
    (1. Ballets – Stories, Plots, etc.) 1. Title.
    ML3930.A2L38   792.8'4   78–24178
ISBN 0–8317–0683–X

Manufactured in Italy
First American Edition

Illustration page 2 shows Sir Frederick Ashton
in The Royal Ballet's production of Cinderella.

Contents

Introduction

Long before you have made up your mind to go to the theatre many people have been at work to create the ballet you are going to see. First there are the dancers, who have trained at a dancing-school like that of The Royal Ballet, the Kirov, the Bolshoi, New York City and American National, the Canadian, Australian or other companies. Some of these dancers have studied for as long as eight years before they begin to dance on stage. Second there is the choreographer, who arranges the dances and the steps and gestures through which the dancers tell the story. Third there is the composer or musician, who works closely with the choreographer, for the music enables the dancers to phrase their movements and give them expression. Fourth there is the artist, who designs the scenery and costumes which help you to understand what kind of people are telling the story, where they live, the time of day, the weather and where the story takes place.

But have you ever thought that even while you are on your way to the theatre these people are still working to ensure that you enjoy the ballet? On stage, or in some large room, the dancers are warming up, for no one dances on stage without preparing their muscles. The stage-hands are setting the scenery and getting the props ready. The electricians are placing and testing the lights. The stage manager and his helpers are seeing all is ready. Downstairs the members of the orchestra are tuning their instruments.

As you come into the theatre and find your seats, the dancers put the finishing touches to their make-up and costumes. The call comes – 'Beginners, please' – and so they go down to the stage. But we, behind the curtain, are not sure you are ready to watch. There is still something more to do. At last the theatre darkens. The conductor taps his desk, then raises his baton.

The music begins. We, on stage, know that it helps us to feel the mood, emotions and actions of the characters we are to dance. We hope that the music will help you, too, to understand what we are trying to tell you. So, in writing these stories, I have tried to tell them as I once danced in some of them or sat, like you, in the audience and watched the curtain go up to take me into the magic world of dance.

Opposite Gradually the ghostly figure of the dead girl rose from her grave in the midst of the forest clearing and she bowed before the Queen of the phantom maidens. Antoinette Sibley of The Royal Ballet in *Giselle.*

La Fille Mal Gardée

The cock was crowing as the peasants stumbled out of bed, rubbed their eyes sleepily, and pulled on their clothes. It was harvest-time, and they had to be out in the fields very early to be sure not to miss a minute of the fine weather.

At Mother Simone's farm the old lady was still asleep, but her daughter Lise was already up and dressed and on her way to work in the dairy. As she came down the farmhouse steps from her room and crossed the yard, she absent-mindedly stirred the bowl of cream she was carrying, thinking all the while of her sweetheart Colas—how handsome, how gallant he was. Remembering that she had promised to leave him a secret message, she took a length of pink ribbon from her pocket and tied it to a nail in the stable wall before disappearing inside the dairy.

Not long afterwards Colas came through the farmyard with his shepherd's crook over his shoulder, for he was off to the pastures to tend his sheep. He stopped a moment, hoping to catch a glimpse of pretty Lise, but he knew that he must not let her crotchety old mother see him, for she thought he was far too humble a suitor for her only daughter, and was always angry when she found him hanging around anywhere near her farm.

Cautiously Colas looked about him, and as he did so, he noticed the piece of pink ribbon fixed to the wall. Delighted that Lise had not forgotten her promise to him, he took the ribbon and tied it to the end of his crook. By this time he was in such good spirits that he could not resist peeping through a chink in the shutters in the hope that he might see Lise. The noise he made disturbed Mother Simone, who flung open the upstairs window and discovered him. Immediately she flew into a temper, stormed out on the balcony in her nightgown and cap, and proceeded to pelt him with anything to hand in order to scare him away. Cabbages, onions, carrots and even a geranium plant came hurtling through the air. Colas quickly took to his heels just before Lise came out into the yard to see what all the commotion was about.

Still angry, the old dame set her the task of helping her to churn the butter, but when Lise by mistake dropped the heavy churn on her foot, she hobbled back inside the farm in pain, leaving her daughter in tears. Immediately Colas, who had not gone off to the fields at all, but had stayed hiding behind the wall, ran to her side. Soon he had made her smile again by playing games and pretending that they were already married. But their tender kisses were interrupted by the arrival of the villagers, who were coming to collect the scythes

The old dame cried with pain as Lise dropped the heavy milk churn on her foot. Ann Jenner as Lise and Brian Shaw as Mother Simone in The Royal Ballet, Covent Garden production.

Opposite Nadia Potts as Lise and Tomas Schramek as Colas in the National Ballet of Canada production with choreography by Sir Frederick Ashton.

Lise and Colas played at cat's-cradle. Ann Jenner as Lise and Mikhail Baryshnikov as Colas in The Royal Ballet production.

they needed to cut the ripe corn. Impulsively Lise decided to accompany them and run away from the farm that instant so that she could marry the man she loved. She was on the point of going when the door opened and her mother came out. When Mother Simone saw what was happening she caught hold of her daughter and dragged the poor girl on to her lap, spanking her soundly for being so disobedient.

Just then the dame heard voices. Looking up, she saw the wealthy vineyard owner Farmer Thomas coming down the lane to the farm with his son Alain. Quickly setting her daughter down, Mother Simone assumed her most gracious of smiles, for she wanted to impress the squire, having decided that his son was just the young man for her daughter to make a prosperous match. Lise stared in curiosity. Alain certainly had a cheerful smile, but he seemed so odd, not at all like her fine Colas. None of his clothes fitted properly and he was so clumsy that every time he moved he looked as though he was about to fall over.

Eventually his father had persuaded Alain to play the part of the chivalrous suitor and to offer the posy of flowers which he carried. But instead of presenting it graciously to the young lady he thrust it awkwardly under her nose, then covered in confusion, hid himself behind his enormous red umbrella. Lise could hardly stop herself from laughing aloud at this absurd youth and was horrified when her mother urged the visitors to stay and watch the harvest being brought home. She could well imagine how tedious it would be to have to entertain two such difficult men, and with ill grace she climbed into the pony-trap which was waiting at the side of the road to ride off to the fields with her mother, Farmer Thomas and his ridiculous son.

Everybody not already working on the land was going to see the gathering of the crop. Even the cock and all the hens went scuttling down the road. Colas bounded along as happy as could be at the thought of seeing his darling girl. He had also brought two bottles of wine, for the end of the harvest was a merry affair, and there was always feasting and dancing afterwards. The rich farmer escorted Mother Simone and Lise in the trap, and a group of village maidens ran behind them, waving ribbons in the air as if they too were holding the reins of an elegant horse-drawn carriage. Last of all came Alain, furiously galloping – sometimes forwards, sometimes backwards – not on a pony, but on his magnificent red umbrella.

Colas arrived first as the workers were cutting the very last sheaves of corn, and by the time the important visitors had driven up, the peasants were assembled ready to greet them. Then the fun began. Everyone took up their positions for the square dancing. To Lise's disappointment Farmer Thomas insisted that she take his son as her partner. Fortunately Alain was so ungainly that he was never in the right place to take her hand, but was always facing in the wrong direction. Colas was quick to seize his chance, and every time that the clumsy youth looked the other way, he caught hold of his sweetheart's hand and gazed fondly into her eyes. At last Alain was so confused that he lost his place altogether, and Lise and Colas came together in the midst of the village girls who whirled round and round with their ribbons in a maypole dance.

When she saw this, Mother Simone was of course very cross, but the clever young people flattered her, persuading her to give a demonstration of her clog dancing, of which she was extremely proud. Soon she was happily tapping her feet in a thoroughly good humour, and before

Even the cock and all the hens went scuttling down the road to see the gathering of the crop. Dancers of the National Ballet of Canada.

Below Mother Simone gave a demonstration of her clog dancing, and soon everyone began to copy her. Ronald Emblen as Mother Simone in The Royal Ballet production.

long everybody joined her, copying her vigorous steps and capering round the maypole.

Suddenly, however, the sky grew dark, there was a flash of lightning, an ominous clap of thunder, and a great storm broke, putting an end to their merriment. The driving wind and rain blew the dancers all over the place, and poor Alain was carried away, high into the air, riding astride his umbrella like a broomstick. The people fled to their homes, but the summer storm ended as suddenly as it had begun, and as the sun came out from behind the clouds, Lise and Colas found themselves alone together and at once took the opportunity to exchange loving kisses.

All too soon Mother Simone found her daughter and hauled her off home. By the time they had reached the farm, they were both rather bedraggled, although Lise had managed to keep herself from being thoroughly soaked by holding a sheaf of corn over her head.

As soon as they were inside the farmhouse, Lise set to drying their damp clothes, while her mother locked the front door firmly and put the key in her pocket. She was determined that her daughter would never again be able to meet impudent Colas. Then, winding a silken scarf around her neck to ward off any cold she might catch after the downpour, Mother Simone sat down to her work at the spinning-wheel. However, all the excitement and the activity of the day had exhausted her and very soon her head began to nod, her mouth dropped open, and she fell fast asleep in her chair, snoring loudly. Quick as a flash, Lise crept up behind her and tried to steal the key, but the old lady awoke. Pretending that she was still feeling damp and cold, Lise danced round the room as if to keep herself warm, persuading her mother to beat time with a small tambourine. Just as she hoped, the rhythmic tapping soon lulled the dame back to sleep, and when she was once more slumbering soundly, Lise pushed at the door with all her might and tried each one of the windows to see if there was any way of escape. But it was hopeless—everything was securely locked.

As she began to despair of ever seeing her beloved again, the top half of the kitchen door was thrust open, and a head peeped over—it was Colas! He dared not come into the room, but Lise stood on tiptoe and he was able to reach down through the gap above the door and lift her in his arms to kiss her. Suddenly they heard the old lady stirring. The girl quickly jumped to the ground and began cavorting around the room. Indeed, she did this in such a lively way that Mother Simone began to think that she must be feverish.

The old dame was fussing about her daughter when there was a rap at the door. The farm labourers had come to receive their wages for their harvest work and also to offer some sheaves of corn to bring luck for the wedding of Lise and Alain. Lise knew that she must escape soon or it would be too late and she would be forced to marry her ridiculous suitor. When the harvesters had completed their business and were leaving the house, she swiftly made ready to run away with them. Mother Simone, however, was not to be fooled so easily. Grasping Lise by the waist, she dragged her inside. Then before anything else should happen to thwart her plans for the profitable match, she put on her best bonnet and set off with all speed to make the final arrangements with Farmer Thomas, making sure, of course, to fasten the door safely behind her.

Wretched Lise was left alone, doing her best not to cry, and imagining what it would be like if only she were married to Colas. She was lost in her daydreams when all at once she gave a start of surprise, as her sweetheart sprang out from the midst of all the bundles of wheat which the peasants had brought. This was too much for Lise, and she immediately began to weep. Colas had just succeeded in wiping away her tears and encouraging her to smile again when they both heard Mother Simone trudging back through the yard. There was no time for Colas to leave. He must hide—but where? They tried to conceal him under the table, up the chimney or in the drawer, but it was impossible, he was far too visible—he would be seen at once if he remained in the kitchen. So Lise hurriedly pushed him upstairs and into her own bedroom.

By the time the dame had unlocked the door and let herself into the kitchen, the room was empty save for her daughter, who was frantically sweeping the floor and looking very flustered. The old lady was puzzled, but had no chance to find out the cause of the trouble, for the marriage would take place shortly, and her daughter must be ready for the ceremony. Mother Simone sent her upstairs to dress herself in her wedding gown, following close behind and locking her securely in her room so that for the last time she would have no way of escaping.

While the bride was still upstairs, all the guests arrived to celebrate the wedding. The lawyer was there with his clerk to negotiate the legal terms and see to the signing of the contract, and Farmer Thomas made his appearance punctually, dragging his reluctant son behind him. The bridegroom had put on his finest clothes—a splendid new suit, top hat, white gloves, a glittering diamond ring, and an enormous flower in his buttonhole. Everything he wore was brand new, except for the old umbrella which he could not bear to leave behind.

As soon as the parents of the bride and groom

had signed the marriage contract, Mother Simone handed the key of the bedroom to Alain and told him to go and fetch Lise. Blushing deeply, he stumbled upstairs, his whole body contorted with embarrassment. At the door he halted—he dared not go in—but all the guests laughed and shouted impatiently, 'Go on—unlock it!' Summoning up all his courage, he turned the key in the lock, pushed open the door, and fell backwards down the stairs with shock. There stood his future bride, smiling blissfully in the arms of her darling Colas.

Horrified by this public disgrace, Mother Simone fainted away on the spot, and the lawyer tore up the contract that instant. Farmer Thomas was absolutely enraged by the shameful behaviour, and his son could only gaze sadly at the magnificent diamond ring. No one else, however, was in the least bit scandalized. All the friends were delighted, for now they were sure that the two lovers would have to be married.

When the old lady recovered, she was at first

Everyone was happy, for now Lise and Colas would be married after all. Marilyn Jones and John Meehan of the Australian Ballet.

very angry and refused to listen to Lise and Colas when they begged her to forgive them. But when she realized that the lawyer's clerk could easily draw up another marriage contract, her good humour returned. At least the scandal would be avoided, her daughter safely married, and she could stop worrying about her and settle down to a peaceful old age. As for Lise and Colas, they danced for joy with all their friends. Simple Alain was happiest of all, for he had not had to go through the painful ordeal of the wedding ceremony, and was at last left alone to amuse himself wih his dearest possession—his red umbrella.

La Fille Mal Gardée, as performed by The Royal Ballet, Covent Garden

This is one of the oldest ballets still danced today and was first produced in Bordeaux by the French choreographer Jean Dauberval in 1789. This was the year in which the French Revolution began, and Dauberval had been sent away from Paris because the director of the Paris Opéra thought his ideas were too modern. Dauberval wanted to tell a story about farmers and peasants, who had never before had a place on the royal stage. The music, too, was very different, for it was made up of folk songs and dance tunes which everyone knew. The story itself is very old, yet as told by Sir Frederick Ashton for The Royal Ballet it has become quite new. Ashton also made the ballet very English, for he used traditional English folk and Morris dances, as well as jokes told by English clowns and pantomime characters since the seventeenth century. The original music was rearranged by John Lanchbery, who used much of Hérold's score of 1828. The scenery and costumes were designed by Osbert Lancaster, the famous English cartoonist. Ashton's version was first produced at the Royal Opera House, Covent Garden on 28 January 1960. Nadia Nerina and David Blair danced Lise and Colas, Stanley Holden was Mother Simone, Alexander Grant the simpleton Alain, and Leslie Edwards played Farmer Thomas.

La Sylphide

All was quiet in the farmhouse kitchen except for the steady ticking of the grandfather clock. It was still dark save for the glow of the embers in the grate, but outside the sky was streaked with the first light of dawn as the sun began to rise over the Scottish Highlands. Two darkened figures lay slumped in armchairs by the hearth. Every now and then they stirred a little in their sleep, troubled by their vivid dreams. James was to be married that very day to his childhood sweetheart. He dreamt not of her, however, but of a mysterious lovely sylph who seemed to flutter around him, her delicate wings trembling, and gazing at him with loving eyes. He had seen her many times before when he was out working. She had flitted through the trees of the glen, but although he had tried to follow her, she always disappeared from view before he could find out who she was. At last it seemed as if she were within reach, but just as she bent to brush his forehead with the softest of kisses, he awoke with a start. By the time he had opened his eyes, the Sylphide had flown away up the chimney.

Beside him his friend Gurn was still fast asleep, dreaming of Effie, the girl who was to marry James, and whom Gurn had long loved secretly. James called him, but before the lad could rouse himself properly, Effie and her mother had come downstairs, happy and excited at the beginning of this special day. Seeing Effie, Gurn, still half-asleep, could think only that he was losing her for ever and desperately seized this last chance to declare his love. The young girl took no notice and instead turned to James, who was gazing sadly out of the window, where he thought he had seen the Sylphide looking at him. Effie reproached him for appearing so sorrowful on this happy day, and James, at the sight of his sweetheart's smiling face, forgot his dream and embraced her affectionately. But they were not alone for long. Soon the people of the village were arriving with their presents to celebrate the wedding.

Everyone was in a joyful mood and had dressed in their most colourful clothes, all except one old beggarwoman in filthy rags, with matted grey hair, who lurked in the corner by the hearth. James, remembering his dream again, turned towards the chimney where the sylph had vanished and caught sight of the old woman. Horrified by the appearance of this ugly crone who had come uninvited into the home, he harshly ordered her to leave at once. The girls, however, were curious and wanted her to tell their fortunes. Kind-hearted Effie took pity and brought her some bread and milk, little realizing that she was Madge, a most powerful witch. In return for the good deed the old woman took her hand and started to tell her what the Fates had in store for her future.

Margot Fonteyn as the Sylphide.

15

'Will my marriage be happy?' asked Effie.

'Yes,' Madge replied.

Smiling contentedly, the girl then asked a question which hardly needed an answer.

'Does James love me?'

To her horror the hag gave a ghastly toothless grin and croaked, 'No!'

As Effie shrank back, pale and trembling, Gurn stepped forward to offer his hand. Madge declared that it was he and not James who loved her sincerely.

James could bear this no longer and drove the beggarwoman from the house. Saddened by this angry scene, Effie went slowly upstairs with her mother and some of her friends to prepare for her wedding.

When everybody had left, James fell to pondering on the beautiful vision which still haunted him, even in the hour before his marriage to a gentle, lovely girl who was devoted to him. Had he really only imagined it? As he stood lost in thought, something moved past the window. In an instant the Sylphide had flown into the room and stood before him, beseeching him to return her love and to follow her into the glen. As James,

Above The Sylphide stood before James, beseeching him to follow her into the glen. Frank Augustyn and Nadia Potts of the National Ballet of Canada.

Below Madge declared that it was Gurn who truly loved Effie. Tomas Schramek as Gurn and Jacques Gorrissen as Madge in the National Ballet of Canada production.

quite enraptured, drew her close to kiss her, they were both startled by a noise—someone was coming. There was not time for the sylph to make her escape, so she sprang lightly into one of the huge old armchairs by the fire, where James hid her from view with a plaid shawl. The next moment Gurn rushed in, convinced that he had glimpsed his friend in the company of another woman. But though he looked everywhere in the room, there was no sign of anyone else, and he decided that he must have been mistaken after all.

Effie came downstairs, radiantly pretty in her bridal veil, and carrying a bouquet of flowers. A few minutes later the guests returned to the farmhouse, and before long the refreshments were served, the bagpipes started to play merry jigs, and the wedding celebrations began. All the young men crowded round the bride, begging her to dance with them. Only James stood apart, still

Opposite La Fille Mal Gardée: Colas was able to steal kisses from Lise when Alain was not looking. Merle Park as Lise, David Blair as Colas, and Alexander Grant as Alain in The Royal Ballet production (see page 10).

thinking of the mysterious creature who had so bewitched him. When Effie admonished him, her own bridegroom, for being the one person to neglect her, he quickly recovered his senses, and the two joined hands in the centre of the dancers. But in the midst of the general fun and dancing, the youth seemed to see the Sylphide, and whirled his sweetheart round and round with him as he tried to catch her. Effie, however, was too happy to notice his strange behaviour.

When the jigs and reels had ended, it was time for the marriage ceremony to be performed. The bridal pair stood together while everyone watched in silence. They were on the point of exchanging wedding rings, when the sylph darted between them and stole the ring from James's finger. All present gasped in horror as he, quite forgetting Effie beside him, rushed out of the house and into the woods after the fairy creature. Poor Effie burst into tears, unable to understand what had happened, while her mother and friends did their best to comfort her. They gently removed her veil and placed the tartan shawl around her shoulders as Gurn, ever true, knelt beside her to assure her that he at least would never cease to love her.

Deep in the gloomy forest, where the branches of the trees were so thickly entwined that the light of the moon could not filter through, a group of aged crones hovered over a smoking cauldron, chanting eerie phrases. In their midst old Madge poked her crooked stick into the bubbling, evil mixture and drew out a long silken scarf. She cackled gleefully then, clutching the precious cloth, disappeared with the other witches into the dense undergrowth.

A new day was dawning, and James had been searching for the sylph for many hours. At last, when he had almost given up hope, she appeared and flew to his side, bringing him a bird's nest, wild strawberries and water from the stream. He was overjoyed to see her, but when he tried to catch hold of her she was instantly surrounded by a host of other delicate sylphs, and remained among them, constantly eluding his embrace.

Opposite James watched helpless as the sylphs lifted the lifeless figure of the fair Sylphide and carried her off above the trees. Anna Laëkersson and Heming Kronstam of the Royal Danish Ballet.

The Sylphide's strength ebbed away as soon as James had placed the magic scarf around her shoulders. Gelsey Kirkland and Mikhail Baryshnikov in the American Ballet Theatre production.

As the bright morning sun rose high over the tree-tops, all the ghostly figures disappeared. James was left alone yet again, tormented by the thought that he would never be able to capture the lovely maiden of his dreams. Just when he had decided that she was nothing more than an illusion, he heard a crackling of leaves and turned to see old Madge emerging from the woods, the magic scarf in her hands.

Recognizing her, he quickly asked to be forgiven his previous rude behaviour, but the witch merely replied that it was of no consequence and asked why he was looking so dejected. When she had heard the cause of his woes, she smiled cunningly and held out the enchanted cloth.

'This is no ordinary scarf,' she told him, 'for I have woven it with magic. If only you are able to wind it round the arms of your beloved, she will never fly again, and shall be yours for ever!'

Delighted, James took it and had just time to thank her before the old crone disappeared into the forest, for she had seen the Sylphide approaching.

As soon as he perceived the lovely sylph floating through the, trees with her companions, James ran after her and finally managed to catch her in his arms. This time she did not instantly slip from his grasp, and he was able to place the magic scarf around her shoulders. At once she gave a piteous cry, her wings fell to the ground, and she collapsed dying at the feet of the horrified youth as wicked Madge let out a hideous cackle of laughter.

Distraught with grief, James knelt beside the lifeless figure of the fair Sylphide and watched helpless as the other sylphs lifted her in their arms and carried her off above the trees. Far away in the valley bagpipes sounded joyfully and church bells rang out to celebrate the marriage of Effie and her faithful Gurn.

La Sylphide, as performed by the Royal Danish Ballet

This romantic ballet was first produced at the Paris Opéra on 12 March 1832 by the Italian choreographer Filippo Taglioni for his daughter Marie, who became one of the most famous dancers of her day. The ballet was taken to Copenhagen and produced at the Royal Theatre on 28 November 1836 by the famous Danish ballet-master Auguste Bournonville, who danced the role of James, with Lucile Grahn, also a Dane, as La Sylphide.

When Marie Taglioni appeared in this ballet, it was the first time that any ballerina had been seen to run and poise right on the tips of her toes, or to wear the light, gossamer costume we call the 'ballerina' skirt. It was also one of the first theatrical events to use the newly invented gas lighting, and the flickering light lent an air of mystery to the making of the magic scarf and the sylphs flying through the air.

The ballet has long been associated with many famous Danish dancers since Bournonville and Grahn, including Margot Lander, and Margrethe Schanne, whose photograph as the Sylphide appeared on one of Denmark's postage stamps. Amongst the most famous of those dancing James was Erik Bruhn.

Giselle

Long ago in Silesia, a land of dark forests and streams, lived a young duke named Albrecht. He had everything that could be desired, for he was handsome and rich, and betrothed to a countess who would bring him honour and more wealth. And yet he was not happy, for one day, passing through the forest where he went hunting with his royal friends, he caught sight of the most beautiful girl he had ever seen and immediately fell in love with her.

'What can I do?' he cried. 'My father will not let me marry a village girl, and besides, she will never look at me, for she will be frightened by my servants and fine clothes.'

For the first time in his life Albrecht cursed his good fortune and wished that he had been born a humble peasant. Then he had an idea.

'I will disguise myself in simple clothes and pretend that I come from a village on the other side of the woods. No one will recognize me, and perhaps I may win the love of this sweet maiden.'

This he did, and was so successful that he had soon made friends amongst the villagers, and Giselle grew to adore him. Only his servant Wilfred knew his secret and constantly tried to persuade him to give up this rash pretence which could only have unhappy consequences, especially since he was already engaged to be married. But Albrecht was too deeply in love to think about the future, and continued to visit his darling girl as often as he could escape from his noble friends at the castle.

One day he arrived as usual outside the cottage where Giselle lived with her widowed mother, but this time he was observed as he took off his fine cloak and sword and handed them to his servant Wilfred for him to hide in a nearby hut. The secret onlooker was Hilarion, who had long loved Giselle and bitterly resented her affection for her new suitor.

As soon as Albrecht had knocked at the cottage door, Giselle ran out, eager to see him, but he hid from view just to tease her. When at length she managed to catch him, she played a game with her sweetheart, pulling the petals from a daisy flower as she chanted the words, 'He loves me; he loves me not.' Seeing how distressed she was when the remaining petals seemed to tell her that he was untrue, Albrecht seized the daisy and quickly proved that he would love her forever. Just at this moment jealous Hilarion burst in to reveal to her what he had seen.

'Be careful,' he exclaimed. 'He is false!'

But Giselle was far too happy to pay any attention to him.

It was the season of the grape-harvest, and all the young people were gathering together to pick the fruit of the vine and enjoy themselves in celebration of their work with dancing and feasting. Excitedly Giselle joined them in their

The young people danced joyfully to celebrate the harvest. Gelsey Kirkland and Mikhail Baryshnikov in the American Ballet Theatre production.

lively dance. She moved so quickly that for a moment she felt a little faint, but she soon recovered in Albrecht's arms and went back to her friends and their celebration. Just then her mother flung open the door of her cottage and was furious to see what was happening.

'Stop!' she cried to her daughter. 'Stop all this dancing or something terrible will happen one of these days, and you'll dance yourself to death!'

A gloomy hush descended over the crowd of villagers after this ominous warning, and they went off to the fields in silence to resume their work as Berthe hurried her daughter inside the cottage and shut the door.

Albrecht, who had just time to exchange a secret kiss with Giselle, now jumped up, for he had heard the sound of a distant horn and knew that meant the royal huntsmen were out and would soon come across him if he did not escape at

once. If they were to find him in his peasant clothes, his secret would be discovered and he would be undone. He managed to get away just as the Prince, his daughter Bathilde, who was promised in marriage to Albrecht, and the rest of the courtiers arrived in the woodland clearing. They had seen smoke coming from the chimney of Berthe's house and had decided to stop and rest there and ask for some refreshment. They had been riding since daybreak and were tired and thirsty.

Wilfred knocked at the door of the cottage and asked Berthe for something to drink. The old lady was flattered to receive such important visitors in her modest home and immediately sent her daughter to attend to their requirements. Soon Giselle brought some wine and poured it for the royal guests. As she handed a glass to Countess Bathilde, she gasped in delight at the richly embroidered cloth of the great lady's dress, and could not resist bending down to feel the material against her cheek. Bathilde was touched by this action.

'How does a pretty girl like you pass the time in

Giselle bent down to feel the rich material against her cheek. Michela Kirkaldie as the Countess Bathilde, Lucette Aldous as Giselle, and Robert Olup as Albrecht in the Australian Ballet production.

such a remote place in the forest?' she asked.

'I spin,' Giselle told her.

'Oh yes I know, but that is your work. What do you like to do best of all?' asked the Countess.

'Why I love to dance,' cried Giselle, and immediately she spun round with the same joyful steps as before.

'Stop, stop!' the great lady entreated her, explaining as Berthe had done what would happen if she continued to dance in such a way.

Poor Giselle was again most upset by these words, so Bathilde, trying to distract her, started to talk kindly to her about other matters. When she discovered that the girl had a sweetheart, she exclaimed, 'Why I too am engaged to be married!' and taking off one of the dazzling necklaces which she wore, she placed it round Giselle's neck as a present. The young girl was quite overcome with joy and hardly was able to thank the Countess, before her mother ushered the noble visitors into her home.

The door had scarcely closed behind them when Hilarion emerged triumphant from the hut nearby where he had just discovered the hidden cloak and sword belonging to Albrecht. Now he could prove that his rival was a lying scoundrel.

Singing and laughing, the young people returned from their work in the vineyards and were now going to devote themselves to the merry-making which followed the harvest. They had chosen Giselle as their queen, and she was lifted high on to their farmcart, where Albrecht crowned her with a wreath of vine leaves. Jealous Hilarion, watching their celebrations, could bear it no longer, and rushed into their midst, denouncing Albrecht as an impostor.

At first they laughed at him and refused to believe what he said, but then Hilarion held up the magnificent sword which flashed in the sunlight.

'This belongs to no peasant!' he shouted.

Seizing the Prince's hunting-horn, which hung at the door of Berthe's house, he blew it with all his might. The door opened and the royal party came out, wondering what the matter could be. At once they recognized Albrecht and were astonished to see him in his poor clothes.

'What does this mean?' they asked. 'Why are you dressed like that?' Albrecht was so confused that he could only try to pretend that it had all just

been a joke. So he smiled at Bathilde, who was looking very perplexed, and took her hand. Wretched Giselle could not understand why he was acting so strangely, and she rushed up to where he stood with Bathilde.

'No—it's not true!' she cried. 'He's going to marry me—he swore he would!'

At this the great lady laughed scornfully and proudly showed her the engagement ring which she wore on her finger.

Horrified, Giselle uttered a cry, tore off the necklace which Bathilde had given her and flung it to the ground. Then she collapsed, sobbing uncontrollably. Nothing that the Countess could do to try to calm her was of any use, for Giselle, mad with grief, seemed to be lost to the world. Her gaze was wild, her hair unloosed, and she ran hither and thither as if she no longer saw anything around her. She did not even take heed of Albrecht when he approached her, but pushed him roughly away.

Suddenly she stumbled over the sword which lay on the ground, and before anybody could stop her, she plunged it into her heart. Too late Albrecht snatched it away, for she was already on the point of death. For a moment she recognized him and tried to run away, but then she fell senseless into her mother's arms. In vain Albrecht attempted to revive her with desperate kisses—she was quite dead. Heart-broken, he snatched up his sword and rushed towards Hilarion, meaning to kill him, but Wilfred managed to intervene and quickly led his master away as all the villagers wept over the cold, still body of their Giselle.

Late that night Hilarion wandered sadly to her grave. It was dark and stormy in the forest clearing. The wind howled, and every now and then the sky was lit up by eerie flashes of lightning. The youth soon grew very frightened, for he remembered the legend of the Wilis, the spirits of girls who have perished for love, who lure young men to their death by forcing them to dance until they collapse from exhaustion. At last he could bear the solitude of the lonely place no more, and he took to his heels. He was just in time, for instantly there floated across the moonlit glade the gossamer-winged figure of Myrtha, the Queen of the Wilis. Her beautiful face and frail arms were deathly pale as she glided soundlessly through the trees and summoned her sisters to rise up from the

ground where they were buried and join her. Immediately they all gathered around the new grave of Giselle, while Myrtha commanded her to arise and take her place amongst the Wilis.

Gradually the ghostly figure of the dead girl appeared and she bowed before her Queen. Then she flew up into the air with her sister spirits, and they soared higher and higher until they disappeared above the topmost branches of the trees, ready to descend on any lone traveller in the forest and wreak their dreadful revenge.

Meanwhile Albrecht was coming along the woodland path with his servant Wilfred, who begged him not to delay in such a place for fear of the phantom maidens. Albrecht, however, would hear none of his entreaties but commanded him to leave. As soon as he was alone, he knelt by Giselle's grave and laid down the flowers he had brought. That instant he seemed to see the form of his beloved flitting through the trees. He jumped up and chased after the figure, but though he searched everywhere, he could not find her. Dejectedly he returned to kneel and pray by her tombstone. He had not been there many minutes when he started round, for he had felt the gentle touch of the girl's hand on his shoulder. Again she

Summoned by their Queen, the ghostly Wilis appeared and floated across the forest clearing. Dancers of The Royal Ballet.

fled away, but this time she soon came back to speak to him, and together they recalled the first happy days of their love, slipping away together through the trees as the sinister creatures appeared again at the edge of the glade.

At last the Wilis could exercise their fearful power, for Hilarion had returned to the graveyard. They seized the youth and spun him round and round in a frenzied dance until he was so weak and dizzy that he no longer knew what he was doing, but stumbled and fell into the lake close by, and was drowned at once.

Eager to find another helpless victim, the Wilis sought out Albrecht and dragged him before Myrtha. He begged for mercy, but she was pitiless, and commanded the Wilis to engage him in their gruesome dance. Giselle, however, could not bear this to happen, and although she must obey her Queen and dance with Albrecht, she did this so gently and lovingly that he was able to continue until dawn, when at last he fell down exhausted. But just as Myrtha thought she had

Giselle arose from her grave and danced lovingly with Albrecht until sunrise. Karen Kain and Frank Augustyn of the National Ballet of Canada.

triumphed, the cock crowed and the bells rang out from the church tower. The power of the Wilis was over for another day, and Albrecht had survived his ordeal through the strength of Giselle's love for him.

Giselle had barely enough time to revive him with tender caresses before she too was compelled to fade from sight with the rest of the night spirits. As she fell once more lifeless into his arms, Albrecht lifted her and gently carried her to her grave. There as the sun began to rise through the trees, she disappeared from view for ever.

Giselle, as told by Théophile Gautier and Vernoy de Saint-Georges

This famous ballet was first produced at the Paris Opéra by the French ballet-masters Jean Coralli and Jules Perrot on 28 June 1841. The story was specially written for Perrot's wife, Carlotta Grisi, a most unusual actress-dancer. The music was written by Adolphe Adam, and it plays an important part in helping everyone to understand the plot. Adam was the first composer to use *leit-motifs* – short phrases of music which are repeated whenever a particular character appears. These phrases, heard whenever Giselle enters, are accompanied by certain dance steps, but they are not always quite the same. As the story progresses, Giselle changes from being a simple peasant girl happily in love, to a distraught, mad creature who has lost her lover, and finally becomes a quiet, sad but loving Wili, or ghost.

There have been many famous Giselles since Carlotta Grisi, for it is a role that every artist wants to perform, showing her as both dancer and actress. Among the most famous have been Anna Pavlova, Tamara Karsavina, Olga Spessivtseva, the two English ballerinas Dame Alicia Markova and Dame Margot Fonteyn, and the wonderful Soviet ballerina Galina Ulanova. Among the most famous Albrechts, following Lucien Petipa, the first dancer of this role, have been Vaslav Nijinsky, the English dancer Anton Dolin and the Soviet artist, Maris Liepa.

Coppélia

Once upon a time, in a small town in the land of Galicia, there lived a strange old man named Doctor Coppélius. Some people said he was mad, others called him a magician, and all the children were rather frightened of him. Nobody knew what went on behind the walls of his tall, narrow house, for he hardly ever came out and never spoke to anybody, but lights had been seen shining through the shutters of an upstairs window late into the night, and peculiar muffled noises came from the room inside.

One bright summer's day, however, the doctor peered out of his upper window and then appeared on the balcony with the most beautiful young lady you ever saw. Not a curl of her glossy hair was out of place, her skin was as flawless as peach blossom, her lips cherry-red, and her eyes sparkled as green as emeralds. She sat perfectly still in her chair, her gaze directed at the book she held, while the old man fussed around her, rearranging her dress. When he had pushed her chair into a prominent position so that all the townspeople could admire her, the doctor concealed himself behind the curtain and waited.

Not many minutes had passed before Swanilda, a pretty girl who lived nearby, came into the market square. When she spied the lovely maiden, she called to her to come and play with the rest of her friends, but the mysterious young lady spoke not a word. Swanilda thought this very rude, and was about to leave indignantly when she heard her sweetheart Franz coming down the street. She decided to hide and watch him, for she was jealous of the strange girl's beauty and wanted to see if he would fall for her charm.

Sure enough, as soon as Franz arrived at the house and saw the maiden on the balcony, he stopped, spellbound, and bowed to her very gallantly. When she took no notice, he boldly blew her a kiss, for he was eager to attract her attention. Then, very slowly and gravely, she inclined her head in his direction and seemed to return his greeting. Enraptured, Franz stood beneath the window gazing up at her and wondering how he could ever meet her, when Doctor Coppélius came out and angrily told him to be on his way.

'How dare you talk to my daughter!' he shouted. 'How dare you make such a scene in a public place! Be off with you at once or there'll be trouble!'

With that he hurriedly pushed the girl on her chair back inside the house and slammed the window shut.

When he had gone, Swanilda emerged from her hiding-place and pretended that she had just arrived and was chasing a butterfly which fluttered across the square. Franz joined the pursuit, caught the insect and triumphantly pinned it to his collar. Swanilda burst into tears and told him how cruel he was, declaring that he obviously did not love her any more since he was only interested in the haughty girl who sat by the upstairs window. Nothing that the boy could say would persuade her that he was still true to her.

As Franz tried to comfort her, a great crowd of people suddenly rushed into the market square from all directions, laughing and chattering. They stopped talking when the Burgomaster stepped forward to make an announcement. He proclaimed that there was to be a presentation of a new bell for the town church and that any young couples who also celebrated their weddings on that day would each receive a purse of gold. Everyone was very excited, except Swanilda, who looked most dejected. The Burgomaster noticed her and asked if she would be one of the lucky ones to be given a dowry, for it was well known that she and Franz were betrothed. Sadly she shook her head and answered that he no longer loved her. As no one believed this, the Burgomaster handed her an ear of corn, telling her how she could prove that her beloved was still faithful to her.

Martine Van Hamel as Swanilda and Clark Tippet as Franz in the American Ballet Theatre production.

'Listen carefully,' he said, 'and see if you and Franz and all your friends can hear the grain rattling inside its husk. If you can, then he is true to you.'

Everybody gathered round but to their astonishment they heard nothing at all. Poor Swanilda started to weep again and rushed away with her friends. Heartless Franz, however, only laughed and stayed with the rest of the townspeople to amuse himself dancing with all the other pretty girls until dusk.

As night fell, the door of the tall house opened, and the old doctor emerged wearing his thick coat, muffler and a top hat. He pulled the front door shut, locked it carefully with an enormous key, which he then put in his pocket, and started to trudge off over the square, leaning on his umbrella.

Just then, some rowdy boys came down the road, saw the old man, and immediately surrounded him, jostling and making fun of him. Coppélius was soon very flustered and lashed out in all directions with his umbrella, which only made the youths laugh the more. At last, when the doctor's patience was quite exhausted, the innkeeper heard the noise, hurried outside, drove the naughty lads away, and suggested to the old man that he accompany him to his tavern for a refreshing drink. Gratefully Coppélius agreed and soon the market-place was quiet and empty.

It was growing dark as Swanilda and her friends made their way home, giggling as they tried to see where they were going in the darkened streets. Suddenly one of the girls tripped over something. Bending down, she found a large key lying on the cobblestones. Everyone was excited.

'Whoever can this belong to?' they whispered to each other. 'We'll have to try every door in town until we find the lock it fits!'

All at once Swanilda had an idea.

'Look – this is the old doctor's house, isn't it? Then it must belong to Coppélius himself. He must have dropped it out of his pocket. Now we'll be able to go in and find out all his secrets!'

Her friends were shocked at this daring plan, but the thought of going inside the mysterious house was so tempting that one by one they agreed. The girls crowded around the door as Swanilda put the key in the lock and turned – it fitted! With great caution she pushed the door open and went inside. Nervously her friends followed.

When Doctor Coppélius had recovered his breath, he collected his belongings together to resume his walk. To his horror he found that the key was no longer in his pocket. He rushed out of the inn and began peering all over the ground in case he had dropped it in the gutter. When he saw Franz, who had just come down the road, he was furious and impatiently drove him away before continuing his search. Just then, he looked up and saw his own front door swinging wide open. Instantly he seized his umbrella, ready to strike at any intruders, and stormed into the house.

Franz meanwhile, having bided his time, appeared once more outside carrying a ladder. He had been trying to think of a way of meeting the strange maiden who was so silent and so carefully guarded by her father and had decided that he would have to climb up to her balcony in secret. Under cover of darkness, he propped the ladder against the wall and began to climb.

It was very dark inside the doctor's house. Once

the girls had crept upstairs, all they could see inside the room were grotesque shapes hanging from the ceiling and the dim outlines of sinister forms, standing or sitting absolutely still in menacing postures. As she felt her way round the room, one of the girls gave a shriek of fright – she had stumbled against the figure of a Chinaman, who immediately began jerking his limbs and shaking his head. But when she looked again, she realized that he was only a clockwork doll. All the fearsome creatures were not monsters at all, but mechanical toys!

'I know,' cried Swanilda at once. 'Let's set all the dolls moving and find out how they work!'

Excitedly the girls ran about winding up the toys, and instantly the stiff bodies were jolted into movement. They flung out their legs and arms and nodded their heads back and forth with rhythmical jerks and odd rattling sounds. Enchanted, the girls started to copy their actions, dancing round the room as if they too were dolls, until the mechanism gradually ran down and all the toys stopped, frozen in movement as before. Disappointed, the friends looked for some other source of amusement, and when they noticed the door which led out on to the balcony, they begged brave Swanilda to open it. At first she dared not, but eventually her curiosity overcame her. She flung open the door and waited to see how the mysterious lady would react.

Nothing happened. Swanilda bowed before her, spoke to her, tapped her on the arm and even shook her, but Coppélia did not move. Exasperated, she went up close and peered into her face. Her friends shrank back in terror, but Swanilda burst out laughing.

'Look!' she cried. 'Her eyes don't even move. She's not reading at all. Why, she's only an old doll like all the others! And to think that stupid Franz has fallen in love with that thing!'

All the girls were convulsed with giggles at the idea, but just then there was a cry of rage. Doctor Coppélius stood shaking with fury in the doorway and brandishing his umbrella. Immediately he chased the girls out of his workshop and they ran down the stairs and out of the house as quickly as they could. All, that is, except bold Swanilda, who had just time to sneak on to the balcony before the doctor came back, muttering angrily to himself, and shut the door behind him.

Coppélius was at last settling himself down in a chair, taking off his outdoor clothes, and looking forward to some peace and quiet, when there was a slight noise, and he turned to see the window being gently pushed open. He started up and watched as Franz jumped down on to the floor and crept stealthily towards the balcony where he was sure to find his adored Coppélia. The doctor caught hold of the lad by the ear and beat him soundly with his umbrella as he struggled to get away. When Franz finally realized that it was useless to resist any more, he confessed to Coppélius that he was in love with his daughter, and that it was only because of her that he had ventured to break into his home.

Hearing this, the cunning old man had an idea. If he could somehow capture Franz's life-force and transfer it to Coppélia, then the wonderful doll really would come alive. Acting quickly, he graciously begged the young man to sit down and make himself comfortable. Then he fetched a bottle of wine and two glasses and offered him a drink. Franz willingly accepted, little knowing that the wine contained a powerful sleeping draught, and not noticing that the doctor was careful not to touch his own glass. In just a few minutes, the boy was sprawled over the table in a deep sleep.

Now at last Doctor Coppélius could perform the experiment of which he had dreamt for many years. His life's work would be complete. Hastily he went to the balcony to fetch the doll, and wheeled her back into the room. Then grasping one of his heavy old books of spells, he eagerly turned the dusty pages looking for the magic formula. Very carefully he chanted the weird phrases, waved his hands in the air, and watched delighted as the maiden blinked, moved her arms stiffly and then stood up, her body still bent over awkwardly. He rushed to straighten her back, and she lurched forward, thrusting out her rigid legs and swaying a little from side to side. The doctor ran behind to prevent her from toppling over, and rubbed his hands with glee as her steps became more confident and her movements smoother, until she was even able to carry out a little dance.

Suddenly she seemed to grow impatient, as she broke away from her master and ran round the workshop, winding up all the toys so that they too started to move. The place hummed with whirring

Above Doctor Coppelius was startled as the doll's steps seemed to grow more confident. Peter O'Brien as Franz, Margaret Barbieri as Swanilda, and John Auld as the doctor in The Royal Ballet production.

machinery. Somewhat agitated by her unexpected display of wilfulness, the doctor persuaded her to return to her dance by placing a Spanish shawl about her shoulders and giving her a fan. This appeared to please her, for she immediately turned her attention to performing a coquettish Spanish dance, and when the doctor handed her a Scottish plaid, she obediently executed a Highland Fling.

The old man was marvelling at her talent and congratulating himself on his brilliant invention when to his dismay she again rebelled and rushed madly around, kicking the precious book on the floor, knocking over the toys and shaking Franz, who despite all the commotion was still slumped over the table, fast asleep. When Coppélius finally managed to catch hold of her, he set her down firmly in the chair, scolding her for behaving so badly. Then he pushed her towards the balcony, opened the door, and stopped aghast.

There was the doll Coppélia, dangling lifeless over the balcony, stripped of her dainty costume. He had been deceived all the time, and the dancing toy had been none other than Swanilda in disguise! Too late he whirled round in fury to seize the impudent girl, for she had just succeeded

Below The Mayor gave the doctor a bag of gold to make amends for the damage which had been done in his workshop. Dancers of The Sadler's Wells Royal Ballet.

The bridal couples stood together and prayed for blessing on their marriages. Christine Beckley as Prayer, and dancers of The Royal Ballet.

in waking Franz, and the two were at that moment making their escape, laughing hugely at Swanilda's clever prank.

After this, of course, the lovers were quite reconciled. Franz was completely cured of his infatuation for Coppélia, and Swanilda could no longer be angry, for she had such fun playing her trick on the doctor. When the day came for the Mayor to present the new church bell to the town, they took their place amongst the bridal couples assembled in their wedding finery to be awarded the promised bags of gold.

However, when it came to the turn of Franz and Swanilda, Doctor Coppélius came out of his house fuming with indignation to complain to the Mayor about all the damage they had done in his workshop. Wishing to make amends, the young pair offered him their purse of gold at once, but the Mayor, who was feeling particularly generous that day, told them to keep it and gave the old man another instead.

After that, everyone was happy. The new bell hung high in the church tower above the square and the doctor went back to his home content, to start his experiments afresh. Swanilda and Franz and all their friends danced and sang for the rest of that day and far into the night to celebrate their wedding, until at last the darkness lifted and dawn arrived to announce the beginning of a new morning.

Coppélia, as told by Charles Nuitter and Arthur Saint-Léon

This charming ballet was first produced at the Paris Opéra on 25 May 1870 by the French choreographer Arthur Saint-Léon, with music by Delibes. It was the last production to be staged before the theatre had to be closed because of the Siege of Paris. It marked a poor period in French ballet, for since so many of the male dancers had to go to the barricades or to the wars, the male parts were played by girls dressed as men, or *en travesti*.

Delibes' music is very important. Not only did he include phrases to mark every entrance and dance of Swanilda, Franz and Doctor Coppélius, he also added folk tunes from Poland and Hungary to make the story seem more real and to fit the Polish and Hungarian folk-dance movements that Saint-Léon introduced. The original story was written by E. T. A. Hoffmann at the beginning of the nineteenth century, when scientists were making the first automatons. His strange tales were also to serve as a basis for the opera *The Tales of Hoffmann* and for the ballet *The Nutcracker*. The first Swanilda was the fifteen-year-old Guiseppina Bozzacchi, whom Saint-Léon chose from the classroom of the Opéra. Sadly, she died shortly afterwards from a terrible fever, as did many Parisians during the Siege.

The Sleeping Beauty

A trumpet sounded throughout the great hall of the palace as Catalabutte, the royal Master of Ceremonies, bustled about amongst the assembled throng, making the final preparations for the royal christening. The King and Queen swept in, surrounded by their retinue of servants, and paused by the cradle of their baby daughter Aurora. While the Queen stooped to kiss the little Princess tenderly, the King beckoned Catalabutte and asked to see the guest list which he had compiled. Well satisfied to see the number of people whose names were marked down, he smiled confidently around at the assembled court, assured that no distinguished personages had been excluded from this important royal occasion.

The King had just ascended the steps to take his place on his gilded throne next to the Queen, when the chief guests were announced. These were no ordinary mortals but the six fairy godmothers of the Princess Aurora, who had come to offer their special gifts to her. The Fairy of the Crystal Fountain, the Fairy of the Enchanted

The Lilac Fairy stepped forward just as Carabosse delivered her fearful curse. Alida Chase as the Lilac Fairy and Ray Powell as Carabosse in the Australian Ballet production.

31

Garden, the Fairy of the Woodland Glades, the Fairy of the Songbirds and the Fairy of the Golden Vine each stepped forward to bestow not simple presents but the gifts of Beauty, Grace, Plenty, Language and Energy to the sleeping child. Then last of all it was the turn of the Lilac Fairy, who came up to the cradle ready to endow the baby with Wisdom. But before she had time to do so, a dreadful roar was heard from without the palace.

The courtiers looked round amazed and whispered to each other in frightened tones. What could this be? What had happened to spoil this happy day? They had not long to wait in suspense, for a page rushed in.

Carabosse arrived in the great black coach drawn by her hideous attendants. Monica Mason as Carabosse in The Royal Ballet production.

'A new guest has arrived.' he cried. 'One you have forgotten to invite—Carabosse, the most powerful and wicked fairy in the land!'

The Master of Ceremonies was horrified. How could he have made such a ghastly mistake? Frantically he consulted his list and found that the name of Carabosse was indeed not there. In consternation he knelt trembling before the King, who was white with rage, and the Queen, who was weeping inconsolably.

A deathly silence descended over the court as Carabosse arrived in her great black coach, drawn by her loathsome rat attendants. She stepped out, her eyes glinting, and rubbing her bony hands together with glee, she cackled ominously.

Everyone tried to persuade her to relent and forgive Catalabutte his careless omission, but the wicked fairy only laughed the more. Plucking out

his hair in handfuls she flung it to her rats, who devoured it savagely.

'I too have come to bring Aurora a gift!' she shrieked.

Horrified at the thought of the evil mischief she would work, the nobles tried to plead with her, but Carabosse continued relentlessly.

'Yes, your daughter will grow up to be the most beautiful princess in all the world. But . . .' and she struck her stick on the floor with a terrible crash, 'Then she will prick her finger and she will die!'

The King, the Queen and all the courtiers were aghast. Carabosse raised her stick and broke into hideous laughter, but just then the Lilac Fairy,

Left Princess Aurora danced with her suitors. She was graceful and lovely as the fairies had promised. Lesley Collier and Derek Rencher of The Royal Ballet.

Below Aurora danced with each of the four princes in turn. Lucette Aldous and Frank Croese in the Australian Ballet production.

who had remained hidden behind the cradle all this time, stood forward and held up her wand against the wicked fairy.

Carabosse stumbled back, as the good fairy proclaimed, 'Yes she will prick her finger, but she shall not die. She will fall asleep, and sleep for many, many years, until one day, a prince will come and wake her with a kiss and she shall be happy for ever afterwards.'

The King and Queen were much relieved by these welcome words, and everyone was happy again, all that is, except Carabosse who was quite furious and disappeared from the palace immediately.

Years passed, and Aurora grew up beautiful and radiant and loved by everybody. When the day of her sixteenth birthday dawned, people came from far and wide to celebrate, especially since her father King Florestan had invited the most handsome princes in the hope that she would choose a bridegroom.

Catalabutte, who had been forgiven his mistake of long ago, busied himself in the royal gardens in his capacity as Master of Ceremonies, seeing that all was in order for the day's festivities. When he spied four old peasant women huddled together in a corner knitting, he was very angry and seized their knitting needles.

'How dare you!' he shouted. 'Don't you know that no pins or needles may be used within a hundred miles of the King's palace? Guards—arrest them and throw them into prison!'

Just then the King arrived, saw what was happening and gave the royal command, 'Off with their heads!' However, the Queen and four princes who had come to pay suit to the Princess persuaded the King not to spoil such a joyful day with anger and execution. The King relented and the old women scurried away just as the guests began to assemble. Peasant girls and boys with garlands of flowers, courtiers in their finest apparel, and the four princes, all gathered in the royal garden to await the arrival of the Princess Aurora.

Soon she came running in with her friends, graceful and lovely as the fairies had promised. The four suitors were quite overwhelmed by her beauty and each offered her a rose and begged to dance with her. Aurora danced with them all in turn, then tossed the flowers carelessly to the

ground, refusing to choose any one of them to be her husband, for she enjoyed her youth and freedom too much to want to make a choice just yet.

She went back to join her friends in their play and dancing, when all at once she noticed a haggard old woman who was spinning in a corner. The young girl was enchanted, for she had never seen such a thing as a spindle, and she picked it up and played with it. The King and Queen, the nobles and all who knew of the dreadful curse were horrified, but before they could stop her, the Princess gave a cry of pain, for she had pricked her finger. She swooned and fell to the ground as her parents rushed to her side.

At this moment the old woman threw off her tattered rags. It was Carabosse in disguise. She uttered a fearful shriek, and then with a great flash vanished in a puff of smoke before anyone could catch her. Amidst general dismay the princes rushed through the garden with drawn swords after the wicked fairy, while the Queen and her ladies-in-waiting collapsed weeping.

Suddenly, from the heart of a glittering fountain there appeared the Lilac Fairy, who raised her wand and declared, 'Do not despair. Aurora is not dead, but only sleeping, and she will sleep for a hundred years. And so will all of you. When she awakes, you shall all awake together, and the spell will be broken.'

Then she waved her wand and everyone—the ladies-in-waiting, the peasants, pages, princes, King, Queen and courtiers all slumped down instantly, wherever they stood, in the deepest sleep. Creepers grew up out of the ground, entwining the trees and the stone statues in the garden, covering the steps and spreading across the palace doors and windows until all the castle grounds had been obscured by a dense, dark forest.

So thick was the undergrowth, so complete the spell, that the palace remained undiscovered in the depths of the woods for many, many years. Then one day, exactly a hundred years later, Prince Florimund and his courtiers were out

Opposite Catalabutte swept into the palace with her fearful servants, and everyone trembled for the Master of Ceremonies had forgotten to invite her to the Christening. Victoria Bertram of the National Ballet of Canada.

hunting. As they galloped through the trees, they saw a woodland glade beside a river, so they stopped to rest and refresh themselves, while the young Prince sat down beside a tree with his tutor.

During the course of their talk, the tutor tentatively brought up the subject of marriage. Although it was certainly time for him to find a wife and produce an heir, and although the ladies of the court were very alluring, Florimund was really not interested, for he had not yet found the girl of his dreams. The tutor organized a game of Blind Man's Buff, but the Prince remained apart, and when the courtiers, tiring of their game, made ready to leave, Florimund urged them to go on without him, leaving him to rest and think.

He had not been alone for many minutes, when there appeared floating down the river a wondrous boat, its sail shimmering in the breeze. On the deck stood the dazzling figure of the Lilac Fairy who asked him to describe his sweetheart. When he replied that no one had yet captured his heart she told the astonished Prince that she would be able to show him the girl of his dreams, whom he had sought for so long. With a wave of her magic wand, she conjured up a vision of the sleeping Princess in the trunk of one of the great oak trees growing in the forest clearing. Immediately Florimund was captivated by her beauty, and begged the good fairy to lead him to her. Then he seemed to see Aurora and her friends dancing before him, but as soon as he tried to embrace her, she disappeared as suddenly as she had come.

Florimund threw himself at the feet of the Lilac Fairy.

'Where, oh where can I find this vision – this lovely girl?' he beseeched her. 'Lead me to her I beg you, I must find her.'

'Come,' said the fairy, and together they stepped on to her enchanted boat and glided off down the river on their magical journey. Autumn leaves fell about them, and frost and icicles sparkled on the darkened branches. Then, in the twinkling of an eye, they left winter behind them

Opposite The wedding of Princess Aurora and Prince Florimund was a magnificent affair, and the most distinguished guests came from far and wide to attend. Christopher Carr as Puss in Boots and Anita Young as the White Cat in The Royal Ballet production.

The glittering figure of the Lilac Fairy emerged from the fountain. Vergie Derman in The Royal Ballet production.

as they sailed further and further into the forest, and the pale sun began to shine through the leaves of the trees, revealing the distant turrets of a great castle. By the time the boat stopped it was high summer, and the Prince and the Lilac Fairy stood before a thick hedge. They alighted from the boat, and as the fairy waved her wand the dense brambles parted, and they were able to find a way through the undergrowth to the massive old door of the castle, which loomed up mysteriously in front of them out of a strange mist. As the fairy touched it with her wand, there was a creaking of rusty hinges, and the great door swung open slowly for the first time in a whole century.

The Prince rubbed his eyes in amazement as the mist gradually dispersed, for as he gazed around him he saw, covered in cobwebs and dead leaves, the motionless figures of courtiers who had fallen asleep just where they stood when the spell had been cast. Fighting his way through the brambles, Prince Florimund followed the fairy through the garden, past guards on duty, princes with swords raised, ladies-in-waiting clustered around the Queen, and the Master of Ceremonies bent over his list, all absolutely still, in the deepest of slumbers. He climbed the steps and went into the palace. He followed the fairy down long corridors,

The spell was broken at last and Princess Aurora and Prince Florimund were married. Karen Kain and Frank Augustyn in the National Ballet of Canada production.

through deserted chambers, and never once did he see a sign of life, not even a mouse poking its head out of a hole in the wainscot.

At last the Lilac Fairy pointed to a door. He pushed it open, and there before him on a magnificent bed covered with silken draperies lay the lovely Aurora, sleeping peacefully. The Prince rushed up to her and shook her, but she did not wake. Desperately he implored the fairy to help him, but she shook her head and refused to say anything. He turned back to the Princess and then, spellbound by her beauty, he bent forward and very gently kissed her. Immediately she

opened her eyes and smiled up at him. The spell was broken at last, and the sleeping palace awoke.

The wedding of Prince Florimund and Princess Aurora was a splendid affair, and there was feasting and dancing for twelve whole days and nights. Everyone in the kingdom took part in the festivities, and guests travelled from far and wide across land and sea to be present. The fairies were there of course, dazzling in Gold, Silver, Sapphire and Diamond, and so were Puss in Boots and the White Cat, the Bluebird and the Enchanted Princess, Red Riding Hood and the Wolf, and many, many more.

This time there was nothing to spoil the enjoyment of the celebrations, and as King Florestan joined the hands of the Prince and Princess together in marriage, the Lilac Fairy hovered above them in the air to give her last blessing and grant them happiness for the rest of their days.

The Sleeping Beauty, as told by Vsevolozhsky and Marius Petipa

This classical ballet was first produced by the French choreographer Marius Petipa at the Maryinsky Theatre, St Petersburg on 15 January 1890. The old fairy tale had been written by Charles Perrault at the end of the seventeenth century and was chosen by Vsevolozhsky, director of the Imperial Theatres, to restore the former magnificence of the Imperial Ballet. He persuaded Tchaikovsky to compose the music, for which the choreographer Petipa first provided a detailed plan. This gave Tchaikovsky all the information he needed to tell the story, such as the number of bars, time signature, tempo and the instruments that he preferred. Above all, this outline showed the composer what each piece of music was supposed to represent.

The ballet has remained in the repertoire ever since; it is a test-piece, not only for the ballerina but also for many other soloists. The first Aurora was Carlotta Brianza. When Diaghilev presented it at the London Alhambra with wonderful scenery and costumes by Bakst, he showed no less than five ballerinas from Russia—Trefilova, Egorova, Lopokova, Spessivtseva and Nemchinova—and among the *corps de ballet* were several English dancers who would later make their names in English ballet—Dame Alicia Markova, Anton Dolin and Errol Addison. Later Aurora became one of Dame Margot Fonteyn's most famous roles, particularly after the Sadler's Wells Ballet had first visited America and she became recognized as one of the world's greatest ballerinas. At the first performance the role of Carabosse was played by Cecchetti, who also danced the Bluebird.

The Nutcracker

The street was cold and dark outside Doctor Stahlbaum's house and a gang of rough lads threw snowballs at an old beggarwoman who lurked near the gutter. Above them, however, laughing voices could be heard and a warm light streamed from the open doorway as guests arrived one after another and were welcomed inside. Last of all came Drosselmayer the scientist—a strange figure in his voluminous cloak and great hat, with a sinister black patch over one eye.

It was Christmas Eve, and all over the little town in Germany families and friends were congregating to celebrate and exchange presents. Clara and her brother Fritz could hardly contain themselves for excitement at the thought of the fun they would have, and of being allowed to stay up late, long past their bedtime. They imagined the wonderful presents they would receive, especially from Godfather Drosselmayer, who was a brilliant inventor and made mechanical toys with such skill that they appeared quite magical. Indeed, their godfather was so clever that he not only fascinated them, but frightened them too, especially with his horrid black patch covering the eye he had lost during one of his stange experiments.

For hours, it seemed, they had been dressed in their best clothes—Fritz in his velvet jacket, Clara in her pretty frock—waiting impatiently for their parents to finish decorating the great Christmas tree which stood proudly in the drawing-room. At last, when they had begun to despair of the party ever taking place, the owl carved on top of the clock flapped his wooden wings, the clock struck nine and all was ready.

The friends and relatives of the doctor and Mrs Stahlbaum were ushered into the drawing-room.

Opposite The clock struck midnight and Clara was suddenly frightened. But then she looked up amazed as the gallant toy soldiers marched across the floor. The Festival Ballet production.

Ecstatically all the children rushed up to the Christmas tree which sparkled with tinsel and flickering candles. Sweets of every description—chocolates, marzipan, caramels and candy, sugar-plums and apricots—hung from its branches, and presents were piled on the floor beneath. At once they tore open their parcels, exclaiming with delight. Tenderly the girls cradled their dolls in their arms and pretended to rock them to sleep, while the boys blew insistently on their tin trumpets and charged round the room as if they were soldiers on horseback, upsetting the old people and threatening to knock everyone over.

There were games to play, more toys to admire and delicious sweets to be eaten. Time passed quickly, and as the wooden owl beat his wings again the door was opened and in walked Drosselmayer. He had brought so many presents that they had to be carried in by a team of footmen, but the children were too scared of him to approach. Gradually, however, they became curious as the old man demonstrated some of his ingenious conjuring tricks. Soon they forgot their fear and crowded round him to see the marvellous toys he had brought. They were all clockwork dolls which he had made himself, each clothed in a different costume—a soldier with his gun, an Eastern dancer brandishing a sword—but everyone laughed in surprise when a stiff little Russian peasant figure turned out to be Clara in disguise.

To the childrens' bitter disappointment, the doctor and his wife decided that these toys were far too valuable to risk being damaged and ordered the footmen to carry them away for safekeeping. Poor Fritz and Clara were very sad not to be able to play with such magnificent presents and it seemed as if all their fun was spoilt. Drosselmayer was quick to notice this, and pulling a large nutcracker from his pocket, he told them that they could play with it as much as they

Clara, delighted with the new toy that her godfather had given her, played with the nutcracker. Merle Park in The Royal Ballet production.

Above Godfather Drosselmayer had brought some wonderful mechanical toys for the children. The American Ballet Theatre production.

pleased. Fritz was scornful of such an odd toy, but Clara, delighted, examined it and listened to the funny cracking sound it made. Immediately her brother became interested and forced an enormous nut into its jaws with such violence that he broke all its teeth. In disgust he threw it down on the floor, but Clara was most distressed, gently picked it up and placed it carefully to rest in her doll's crib.

When they saw this, the boys roared with contemptuous laughter and began to tease all the girls, making such a dreadful noise that the doctor decided to put an end to it by engaging all the older guests in one of the traditional dances which reminded them of their youth. Everyone enjoyed this, but the most aged among them were so weary by the time it was finished that they had to be helped to their seats, for they were utterly exhausted.

It was indeed very late by now, and the guests began to take their leave, thanking their hosts for the happy evening they had spent. Fritz had suddenly felt so tired that he had fallen asleep in a chair and was carried out, still sleeping soundly. Clara, thinking all the time of her poor injured nutcracker, wanted to take it up to bed, but her parents told her to leave it where it was. So she tucked it up carefully, whispered goodnight, and went upstairs.

The house was quiet and all was dark and still in the deserted drawing-room, when Clara crept downstairs again in her nightgown and pushed open the door. She was far too excited to sleep and simply had to come and see if her dear nutcracker was safe. She had never been in the room all alone at night before. It looked so different, full of threatening shadows, and she was already feeling nervous when suddenly something flapped in front of here, seeming to stare at her out of the darkness. The clock struck midnight. Too frightened now to run away, she heard the squealing and scratching of rats behind the walls and under the floorboards. The noise was getting louder every minute and the Christmas tree appeared to be growing before her very eyes as she sank down fearfully into a great armchair and huddled among the cushions.

'Who goes there?' a voice called. Looking up, Clara saw a gallant army captain go marching across the floor, followed by soldiers pulling a cannon and more troops on horseback. To her horror an army of rats now emerged from their holes and scuttled up to the tree where they devoured the dainty sweets hanging on the branches, and gnawed viciously at the dolls which had been left behind by the girls. The soldiers challenged them, and a terrible battle ensued. Soon nearly all the troops, despite their valiant efforts, had been eaten alive. Terrified, Clara saw the evil rodents come rushing towards her. She jumped up and ran off round the room, but they seized hold of her nightdress and dragged her back. Desperately she scrambled on to the chair and was trying to push them away, when out from the cradle leapt the nutcracker in the form of a handsome Prince. Breathless with admiration, the little girl watched as he fought her assailants single-handed until they had all been killed or had run away in terror. Only their leader remained. Then King Rat and Nutcracker Prince faced each other and began their fight to the death.

Clara could not bear to see her brave Prince

The magical snowflakes whirled in the air as Clara was transported in an enchanted boat to the Kingdom of Sweets. Dancers of The Royal Ballet.

Clara was enchanted to see the little Chinese Acrobats who represented Tea. The Festival Ballet production.

overcome by this wicked monster, and taking off one of her slippers, she flung it with all her might at the Rat King. The blow knocked him down instantly, and with that the rat forces were entirely defeated.

Taking Clara in his arms, the Prince thanked her for performing such a courageous deed, and invited her to accompany him on a journey to the Kingdom of Sweets. Eagerly she agreed and at once the room was filled with a whirling storm of snowflakes which grew larger and larger until the room disappeared completely. They were no longer in the house at all but sailing down an enchanted river in a ship of sea shells.

The little girl could hardly believe her eyes when they arrived in the magical Kingdom, for she was surrounded by the most exotic sweetmeats of every kind. Fountains flowed with orangeade,

lemonade and fruit juices of all flavours. Sweet delicacies from lands far and wide and fairy-tale characters came to life to entertain her. A lively group of Spaniards brought her Chocolate, little Chinese acrobats represented Tea, and the Coffee dancers came all the way from Arabia. Clara clapped her hands in delight to see the fragile sticks of sugar candy and laughed aloud at Mother Gigogne, the old woman who lived in a shoe, whose many children all popped out from underneath her skirts. Rapturously she watched

Opposite Most wonderful of all in the Kingdom of Sweets was the Sugar Plum Fairy herself as she danced with the Nutcracker Prince. Carol Hill and Nicholas Johnson of the Festival Ballet.

Overleaf The Sleeping Beauty: the King and Queen were horrified as Aurora swooned and fell to the ground. Antoinette Sibley as Aurora, Gerd Larsen as the Queen, Leslie Edwards as the King and Alexander Grant as Carabosse in The Royal Ballet production (see page 34).

as the marzipan sweets of delicate green, pink and gold waltzed together like beautiful spring flowers.

But most wonderful of all was the Queen of the Kingdom, the Sugar Plum Fairy, who now appeared clad in the glittering pink of sugar crystals. She was none other than Clara herself. The Nutcracker Prince took her hand and together they danced with magical grace, as all the sugar fairies spun round them in dazzling array.

Suddenly the sky began to grow dark, and horrible creatures like rats and bats appeared.

Opposite Coppélia: Doctor Coppélius cast his spell and was delighted as the doll rose stiffly to her feet and began to move forward with jerky steps. Dancers of the Royal Ballet School in a performance at Covent Garden (see page 28).

The Coffee dancers came all the way from Arabia. Vergie Derman, Alexander Grant and Julian Hosking of The Royal Ballet.

What was happening to the enchanted Kingdom? Clara tried to push them away, and as she did so she opened her eyes to find that she was still sitting in the chair and the party was just drawing to a close. The dreadful monsters were only the guests bending over to bid farewell.

Drowsily the little girl stumbled to her feet, catching sight of the tin soldiers which were scattered on the floor beneath the tree and of the nutcracker which lay where she had placed him in the cradle. Some of the other children were fast asleep and had to be carried home. Once more the front door stood open as the friends departed and went off to their carriages. Clara waved to them all as they left until only Godfather Drosselmayer remained. They said goodbye, and as he walked away he turned to give her a curious look before he too trudged off into the snow. Had it really been nothing but a dream?

The Sugar Plum Fairy danced with her Nutcracker Prince. Laura Young and Woytek Lowski in the Boston Ballet production.

The Nutcracker, as told by Petipa, and later by Nureyev for The Royal Ballet, Covent Garden

This Christmas story was first produced by the Russian choreographer Lev Ivanov at the Maryinsky Theatre on 17 December 1892. The director of the Imperial Theatres, Vsevolozhsky, based his brief outline of a plot on the story 'Nutcracker and the King of Mice' by E.T.A.Hoffmann and again persuaded Petipa and Tchaikovsky to work together. But neither man was very enthusiastic, so when Petipa fell ill, his assistant, Lev Ivanov, had to work out the best way in which to present this very difficult story in dance. This was far from easy, because by the end of the first act the whole story was told, so the second act could only be a long series of dances. The ballet undoubtedly lives on today because of the wonderful music by Tchaikovsky and the interesting use he made of the instruments of the orchestra, especially the celesta, which was used for the first time in a serious score. Since its first production there have been many versions, each choreographer trying to make sense of a tale which is in fact made up of several different episodes, but it is always popular as a Christmas entertainment.

Swan Lake

It was Prince Siegfried's birthday, and he and his friends were holding a small party in the palace garden before the great formal ball which was to take place in celebration the next day. There was plenty to drink, and the old tutor who had come to keep an eye on the proceedings was soon a little unsteady on his feet. Everyone was in a cheerful mood, and when some peasants passed by outside the gates, the young men called to them to come and join the fun. The tutor, eager to show that he was not too aged to enjoy himself, whirled round in a dance with one of the girls. But his head began to reel, and he had to sit down, much to everybody's amusement.

The party was growing more and more lively when the Queen came down the steps and into the garden. Somewhat displeased that her son should be amusing himself in such an irresponsible way on the very day of his coming-of-age, she reminded him of the seriousness of the occasion, and told him that the following day he would be expected to choose a wife from amongst the assembled princesses and duchesses at the ball. Then she swept away to the palace with her ladies-in-waiting, leaving the Prince despondent at the thought of the serious duties which lay ahead of him. The peasants' joyful dancing no longer diverted him, and even when his friend Benno suggested that they go off hunting in the forest as soon as it was dark, he did not seem very interested. However, he could never resist the idea of a daring scheme or adventure. Soon he was quite excited by the idea of a moonlit hunt in the woods before the pomp and ceremony of the next day, and he picked up his crossbow and set out with his friends.

They had not been walking long through the forest when they reached the lake. Deciding that this was the very spot to lie in wait for a flock of wild swans to settle on the water, they went a little way off and hid in the undergrowth, leaving Siegfried alone to stay in the glade and watch.

It was absolutely quiet, the waters of the lake were still, and clouds drifted slowly across the sky. Suddenly in the distance he heard a great beating of wings, and looking up, he saw a flight of snow-white swans coming to land in the clearing. Overjoyed at his good fortune, he raised his bow to his shoulder and was just taking aim at the leading bird when he hesitated. He had never seen a swan more graceful. Transfixed, he watched as she came to rest on the shore and then gasped in amazement. She was surely no ordinary swan at all, but a most beautiful maiden. He rubbed his eyes and looked again. Her flowing movements were those of a bird, but her lovely face was that of an enchanting girl, and on her head she wore a golden crown.

Without thinking, he moved forward quickly to catch her, but she darted away. When he had eventually trapped her so that she could not fly from him, she remained quivering with terror, and gazing with wild eyes at his crossbow. Understanding the cause of her fright, he laid down his weapon and assured her that he could no longer dream of harming her in any way. Hearing this, the swan maiden told him that her name was Odette and explained that she was indeed no bird, but a girl who had fallen under the power of a wicked magician, Von Rothbart, who had turned her into a swan and doomed her to remain for ever on the lake. Only in the hours of darkness between midnight and dawn could she resume her human shape. Siegfried begged her to tell him how she could be freed from this dreadful spell.

'There is one way alone,' she replied. 'If, in the short time each night when I am again a woman, a young man should swear to love and marry me, then should I be free again.'

The Prince, who had been enraptured as soon as he caught sight of her, did not hesitate to reply.

'I am that man—I will save you, for I love you and swear to marry you, no matter what power this evil man may wield.'

Anthony Dowell of The Royal Ballet as Prince Siegfried.

At that moment a hideous bat-like figure appeared on a rock at the edge of the lake—it was Von Rothbart himself. Immediately the Prince seized his weapon and was about to fire an arrow at the magician when Odette stopped him, for she knew that his terrible power could never be broken that way. There was a clap of thunder and Von Rothbart made a menacing gesture towards the lovers before disappearing in a cloud of smoke. Then Odette took the Prince by the hand and led him gently away from the lake as a whole host of swans flew down to the ground, beating their wings and arching their slender necks.

At the sight of all these birds, the huntsmen who had been hiding in woods rushed forward ready to shoot. But before they could do so, Odette rose in front of them and implored them to stop, explaining that these were not real swans but maidens, imprisoned as she was by the dreadful spell.

Siegfried stayed with the Swan Princess for as long as he could, vowing to be faithful to her and longing for the time when she should be freed from the magician's curse. All too soon the sky grew lighter, and as the dawn began to break the swans flew away. Odette lingered beside her lover, but Von Rothbart appeared once more, commanding her to return to his kingdom. She

Above A flock of graceful swans flew down beside the lake. Dancers of The Royal Ballet.

Below The little cygnets danced together. Anita Young, Marilyn Trounson, Susan Lockwood, and Rosemary Taylor of The Royal Ballet.

soared up into the sky, and the Prince stood sadly watching her fly further and further away until she had vanished from his sight altogether.

By the time Siegfried and the other huntsmen had arrived home after their night's adventure, the sun had already risen and the palace was bustling with activity. All that day preparations were being made for the ball that was to be held there. The state apartments were scrubbed and polished, decorated with flowers, and an array of wonderful dishes was prepared for the banquet. Princesses, countesses and ladies all over the realm and in neighbouring lands spent hours adorning themselves in their finest gowns and jewels, for each wanted to appear more beautiful

The Prince was bewitched by the dazzling beauty of the stranger. Martine Van Hamel as Odile and Jonas Kage as Prince Siegfried in the American Ballet Theatre production.

than the rest and to be chosen as the Prince's future bride.

At last everything was ready. Shortly after sunset, when hundreds of candles lit up all the windows of the palace, the first guests drove up to the great entrance gate of the royal estate in their carriages and on horseback. When the Queen saw how many charming girls had been brought to the ball she was well satisfied, thinking that from such a gathering her son would be bound to find one who would please him. In the gallery above the guests the musicians started to play and the dancing commenced. Siegfried was presented in turn to each of the loveliest ladies and danced with them all, but to his mother's displeasure, he seemed completely unmoved by their charms and gazed listlessly into the distance as if his thoughts were far away.

Suddenly a trumpet sounded and some late guests were announced. A distinguished-looking gentleman—very dignified and magnificently dressed—strode into the room with his daughter. Siegfried at once smiled joyfully. There surely was his adored Odette, as beautiful as before, but instead of the simple white feathers in which she had first appeared, she was now clad in dazzling gold and black. He rushed to her, and remained close by her side for the rest of the evening, unaware that she was not Odette at all, but Odile, the daughter of the wicked magician. Von Rothbart knew that if he could trick the Prince into betraying the promise he had made to the Swan Princess, then Odette would die and his dreadful curse would be complete.

Spellbound by the glittering beauty of this new guest, who resembled Odette in all respects except in the way she danced proudly before him, Siegfried did not even notice when the Swan Princess appeared in a vision, beseeching him to remember his vow to her. His mother, contented at last, congratulated him on his wise choice. The mysterious young lady seemed to be as rich as she was fair. Without delay Von Rothbart urged the Prince to declare his love and swear to marry his daughter. Puzzled by his strange insistence, the young man nevertheless did so. Instantly there was a crash of thunder, a cry from the abandoned Swan Princess, and a ghastly shriek of triumphant laughter as the magician and his daughter revealed their true identities. Distraught with

Above The Queen was delighted at her son's choice of a bride who seemed to be rich as well as fair. Frank Augustyn, Patricia Oney, and Nadia Potts of the National Ballet of Canada.

Below The swans clustered around the Swan Princess as she danced once more with Siegfried. Merle Park as Odette and Anthony Dowell as Prince Siegfried in The Royal Ballet production.

grief when he realized what he had done, Siegfried at once rushed out of the palace towards the forest in search of Odette.

The swans clustered round their Princess at the side of the lake. She was resigned to her death, but could not bear to think that the Prince had betrayed her. The swan maidens tried to assure her that he had not meant to deceive her – he had been a victim of Von Rothbart's cruel trick.

Once more a terrible storm descended upon the forest. Black clouds scudded across the sky, the water of the lake was dark and forbidding, and thunder and lightning shook the trees until it seemed that they would come crashing to the ground. The magician was again using his evil power in an attempt to prevent Siegfried from reaching Odette. But the Prince's love was strong enough to overcome even that dreadful magic. Eventually he found her and threw himself at her feet begging her forgiveness.

Immediately Odette pardoned him, but sadly told him that she could not escape her fate. She must perish as Von Rothbart had decreed. Only in dying would she be released from his dreadful curse. At once the Prince made up his mind. He would die with her, so that he could follow her and remain with her for ever. The fearful bat-like form of Von Rothbart loomed up in front of them as he tried to prevent their final act of defiance, but he was too late to stop them. The lovers embraced one last time, then plunged into the waters while the magician lay writhing in agony on the ground, his evil force gone, destroyed by the power of true love.   Swiftly the storm clouds departed, the wind ceased to howl and the sky lightened. The tempest had abated and the forest was at peace once more. The swan maidens sank to the earth, folding their wings pathetically as they mourned their dead Princess. But as they looked through the mist that lay over the lake, they saw in the distance a wondrous ship. There stood Siegfried and Odette, clasped in each other's arms as they sailed slowly away to the land of perpetual happiness.

Swan Lake, as told by Petipa and Ivanov

This lyrical ballet was first produced in its present form at the Maryinsky Theatre, St Petersburg on 15 January 1895 by the Russian choreographers Petipa and Ivanov. It had first been produced at the Bolshoi Theatre, Moscow in 1877, but was not a success, largely because Tchaikovsky received no help from the ballet-master with this, his first score for ballet, and everyone agreed that some of the music was difficult for dancers. Unfortunately Tchaikovsky died before he could rewrite the score for St Petersburg, and it was at a concert in his memory that Lev Ivanov, Petipa's assistant, staged the now famous Act II, 'The Flight of the Swans'. This scene was such a success that Petipa and the conductor Drigo were ordered to re-stage the whole ballet, but on no account were they to alter Ivanov's beautiful 'Flight of the Swans'. So they set to work, changing some of the music and using other pieces that Tchaikovsky had written for the piano. They also decided that Ivanov would have to create the dances for the last act, for the music did not suit Petipa's ideas for a finale, when everyone should come on for the last time. So today we see the work of two choreographers – Petipa, for Acts I and III with plenty of *divertissements,* and Ivanov, for Acts II and IV, or the scenes of the swans.

Many ballerinas have danced the role of Odette-Odile since Pierina Legnani, the very first ballerina to dance the difficult thirty-two *fouettés rond de jambe en tournant* a feat of virtuosity that today is expected from students during their last year at any professional ballet school. To be able to dance these steps is a test of technique, but the role of Odette-Odile is more than that, for the ballerina must prove she can act – first as the sad Swan Princess, and then as the glittering, wicked Odile, daughter of the magician, Von Rothbart.

Opposite Prince Siegfried was enchanted by the beautiful creature who had the grace of a swan and the loveliness of a girl. Natalia Makarova and Donald MacLeary in The Royal Ballet production.

Les Sylphides

The moon shone softly through the trees, casting a dappled light over the sombre forest glade. The leafless trees swayed gently in the wintry breeze, and the lofty arches of the ruined monastery rose dimly through a chill mist. Further off a crumbling tombstone lay half buried amongst the trailing branches.

All at once there appeared through the darkness the fluttering white forms of the phantom maidens who hover around the graves of their departed lovers, haunting the lonely woodlands each night until sunrise. So frail were these Sylphides, clothed in fine gossamer, their gauzy wings shimmering, that sometimes it seemed as if they were not creatures at all. One moment they drifted sadly across the clearing like wisps of cloud, the next they whirled round as snowflakes in a blizzard. At length their trembling arms were stilled, their feet came to rest on the earth, and they stood motionless, clustered around the edge of the glade, while a single figure began to waltz all alone to the unearthly strains of a sweet melody which echoed through the trees.

Freed from the tormenting passion of human love, she remembered only its happiness. Her mood of perfect joy was taken up by another sylph, who bounded forth, leaping yet more rapturously, but with an effortless grace, as if her frail body were impelled by some supernatural power.

Just then there emerged from the shadows a young man, clothed in the velvet jacket and ruffled shirt of an age long past. His hair fell in curls to his shoulder, and his sighing pensive air proclaimed his sadness as he wandered through the clearing. It seemed as if he must search for something which he feared never to find. His steps

became more urgent and he ran back and forth, leaping and turning, desperately seeking his lost love.

A dreamy figure glided through the trees amongst her fellow sylphs as if she did not see them, pausing every few steps to listen in rapt attention for some ghostly call in the distance. As she went her way, the young poet returned, and at last he was not alone, for there flew into the glade the spectre of his dead sweetheart. The two lovers danced among the ruins as they might have waltzed long ago in some ancient ballroom. In perfect harmony they moved, but with an intense sadness which was more than mortal beings could bear, for they were only together as phantoms for the short while before daybreak. The sylph flew higher and higher, the poet gently restraining her, until at length she soared away, out of his

Below A Sylphide emerged from the shadows and began to waltz all alone to the unearthly music. Lesley Collier in The Royal Ballet production.

Opposite Swan Lake: two late guests arrived at the ball, a distinguished-looking gentleman and his dazzlingly beautiful daughter. Merle Park as Odile and Derek Rencher as her father in The Royal Ballet production (see page 54).

Above The fluttering white forms of the phantom maidens appeared from the trees. Dancers of The Royal Ballet.

Below A young man wearing clothes of an age long past wandered sadly through the clearing. Alain Dubreuil of The Royal Ballet.

A dreamy figure glided through the trees. Tamara
Karsavina in the original Diaghilev Ballet production.

The sylph flew down to the poet and the two lovers danced together amongst the ruins. Natalia Makarova and Anthony Dowell in The Royal Ballet production.

reach, and was gone. The glade lay deserted in the frosty moonlight.

A few moments later the white maidens came back to dance together once more, their wings quivering, like a host of pale butterflies. Faster and higher they flew over the ground in a flurry of whiteness like the spray of a wave breaking upon the shore. Suddenly the first bird of the new day began to sing and they stopped, frozen still, their shadowy forms growing fainter and fainter until they disappeared altogether into the thin air of the morning.

Les Sylphides, as told by Fokine to music by Chopin

This 'romantic reverie', which was Fokine's name for his ballet, was first produced in St Petersburg on 20 March 1908. Shortly afterwards, on 6 April, it was again performed, this time in the version which is now used, by students graduating from their last class at the famous Maryinsky School. It was then called *Chopiniana* and had been staged in memory of Chopin. When Diaghilev decided to take a Russian ballet to Paris, he renamed the ballet *Les Sylphides* in memory of all the sylphs and wilis of the early romantic ballets which had been staged there and had made so many ballerinas famous. He persuaded the artist Benois to design the mysterious scenery and costumes and he himself arranged the lighting so that the dancers appeared to be lit by moonlight and the whole scene shrouded in a soft mist. In those first performances there were three of the greatest dancers of their day—Anna Pavlova, Tamara Karsavina and Vaslav Nijinsky. Since then most leading dancers from all over the world have performed the roles, for it is one ballet which is danced by every company that wishes to be considered of importance. Although the steps are simple, it is a difficult ballet to dance, because every movement has to be in precise time to the music and yet the dancers must appear to float ever onwards without pause.

The Firebird

There was once an enchanted garden, hidden away behind a high stone wall in the depths of a forest. At night strange noises could be heard as the leaves rustled in the breeze and a great bird beat its wings and called overhead. Nothing could be seen, save for the fruit of a golden apple tree, glowing in the darkness.

One day, as the sun began to rise over the trees, a figure appeared on top of the wall. It was young Prince Ivan, the Tsarevitch, who had come out to spend the day hunting. He had ventured further and further into the forest, no longer knowing where he was, until he had come to the high wall. Unable to resist the temptation of climbing it, he was astonished when he reached the top and saw the garden beneath him, for he had never

The Firebird struggled in vain to escape from Ivan. Tamara Karsavina and Adolph Bolm in the original Diaghilev Ballet production.

expected to find such a place in the heart of the forest. Suddenly there was a flash of brilliant colour, and a wonderful bird flew past him, her glittering plumage shining fiery red. As soon as Ivan had jumped down to the ground, the marvellous creature soared above the garden again. Quickly taking aim with his bow, the Prince tried to shoot her, but her feathers were so bright that they dazzled him, and she flew away out of his reach.

When he found that the bird had disappeared, he decided to explore his surroundings, for he was eager to discover more of the mysterious garden and to find out who owned it. However, he had not had long to look about him before he saw the strange creature returning. This time he was determined that he would catch her, so he hid himself behind the apple tree. She swooped down towards the glittering fruit and plucked an apple. As she did so, Ivan stepped out from his hiding-place and trapped her in his arms. She turned and twisted frantically to try to escape, but no matter how much she struggled he held her securely.

Then the bird spoke to him, begging him to release her.

'I am the Firebird, she who can never die.'

Hearing this, and moved to pity at the sight of the poor creature's struggles, Ivan let her go. Immediately the Firebird pulled one of the scarlet feathers from her wing.

'If ever you are in need, you have only to wave this feather, and I will come to your aid', she told him. Then she rose in the air and was gone.

The Tsarevitch stood alone, feeling rather bewildered in this strange place and wishing the bird had not left him so quickly. He was filled with curiosity and longed to ask her many questions.

He looked up, peering through the trees after the Firebird, and that moment he saw twelve graceful maidens winding their way out of the forest and in through the garden gates. They gathered by the magical tree and were joined by their Princess, who was yet more lovely than all the rest.

Ivan gasped in delight at her beauty, then quickly stepped back into the shadows to watch as the girls clasped hands and danced round the tree, shaking the golden fruit down and throwing

it to one another. When it was the Princess's turn to throw her apple, the Prince could no longer restrain himself, but came out from his place of hiding and caught it. The startled maidens shrank back in fear, but he quickly showed that he meant no harm by taking off the cap which he wore and bowing low before them.

As she took the fruit which he held out to her, the Princess blushed deeply, wondering who this handsome young stranger could be. Then, while Ivan and the Princess gazed at each other, the girls started to dance around them, bringing them gradually closer together in their midst. Spellbound, Ivan drew the Princess towards him and kissed her. At this she sprang back in alarm, warning him that he must leave at once, for the garden belonged to a wicked magician named Koschei, who would surely kill him if he found

A host of evil goblins rushed into the garden and seized the Prince. David Drew as Prince Ivan in The Royal Ballet production.

dragged along the ground behind him as he moved. It was the magician himself, Koschei.

There was an ominous hush and everyone trembled, for they knew the power of his evil magic. Koschei commanded Ivan to kneel at once, but the Prince refused. So the magician tried to overcome him by weaving a sinister spell, but Ivan spat in his eye, for he was a brave youth and knew that he had done no wrong. At that Koschei flew into a terrible rage and raised his stick ready to cast an even stronger spell. The Prince staggered back and nearly fell to the ground.

Then he remembered the Firebird's feather. Only this might save him. He pulled it from his tunic and waved it high in the air. Instantly the bird was at his side. She beat her wings until Koschei's goblins set Ivan free, backing away from

Above Last of all a hideous old man appeared. It was Koschei, the wicked magician himself. Adrian Grater of The Royal Ballet.

him there. But the Prince refused to go, for he had already fallen passionately in love, and resolved never to leave without her.

Suddenly a harsh noise echoed through the trees. The frightened girls ran away through the gates which closed after them, and a black cloud enveloped the garden. Ivan tried to climb the wall, but it was too high: he was trapped. Then he remembered the great iron gates. He flung himself at them and rattled them desperately. They burst open with a dreadful crash; the forest blazed with light, and a host of evil-looking demons and goblins rushed into the garden. Seizing the Tsarevitch, they held him prisoner. As he fought to free himself, the twelve maidens returned, accompanied by more fearsome guards. Last of all there hobbled in a very old, bent man, leaning on a gnarled stick. He was as thin as a skeleton and his long white beard and dishevelled hair trailed to his bony knees. His hideous nails were like claws and his heavy cloak encrusted with jewels

Below Margot Fonteyn as the Firebird in The Royal Ballet production.

her in terror. Then she whirled around the garden, and everyone followed her, bewitched by her magic and unable to do anything but dance wildly until they fell down dizzy and exhausted. Soon they were all fast asleep, and Ivan alone remained awake, staring at the motionless bodies around him and marvelling at the mysterious power of the wonderful bird. But she called him insistently and tugged at his sleeve.

'Quick, Ivan,' she said. 'You must go and search under the roots of that tree. There you will find a casket, and inside the casket you will see a large egg.'

The Tsarevitch looked puzzled, but the bird explained.

'That egg contains the soul of Koschei. In order to destroy the spell and free your Princess from his curse, you must break it into a thousand pieces. But hurry. His power is great, and I cannot keep him asleep for long.'

Ivan rushed to the tree and found the casket just as the Firebird had described. As he raised the lid, the slumbering bodies at his feet stirred uneasily in their sleep. Then he grasped hold of the egg, threw it up and caught it. Immediately the sleepers awoke and rose to their feet, while Koschei trembled with fear and begged him to spare his soul. In desperation the magician clutched at the precious egg. But Ivan laughed aloud and threw it high into the air as he took the hand of the beautiful Tsarevna. The egg smashed to the ground with a thunderous crash and broke into a thousand pieces. The evil spell was broken at last and the garden was plunged into darkness.

A week later there was great celebration at the Tsar's palace. The twelve maidens were married to twelve handsome knights. Then they gathered with courtiers and guests from all over Russia to rejoice at the wedding of Ivan and the beautiful Princess, and to pay homage as they were crowned Tsar and Tsarina of all the land.

As for wicked Koschei and his evil goblins, they had vanished completely. And although Ivan and his Queen often walked in the forest, they could not find the enchanted garden nor the wondrous Firebird. They searched for many hours, but the bird and the garden had disappeared completely, and from that time hence were never seen again.

The Firebird, as told by Fokine for the Diaghilev Ballet

The story of *The Firebird* is based on a number of Russian folk tales. These tell of the immortal bird who represents love and life, the Koschei who represents Death and Evil, an enchanted Princess, and the youngest son of a family. This boy has been sent out to find his own way in the world and of course, after some trials, always wins the Princess. It was first produced by the Russian choreographer Fokine for the Diaghilev Ballet at the Paris Opéra on 25 June 1910. This was the first ballet music composed by Stravinsky with the help of Fokine, who sat by his side mapping out the movements he wanted and singing snatches of folk tunes which set the rhythms. As a result you can hear several favourite Russian folk tunes which represent the hero and the Princess and her maidens. But out of those tunes Stravinsky composed mysterious music, some of which soars upwards whenever the immortal Firebird dances, but forever seems to sink downwards for the entrance of the Koschei and his terrible servants. When the ballet was first produced, the scenery and costumes were designed by a famous Russian artist and designer, Korovin, but later these were redesigned in old peasant style by the artist Natalia Goncharova. The Firebird, although first intended for Anna Pavlova, who refused it because she did not like the music, was marvellously danced by Tamara Karsavina. Fokine himself danced the Tsarevitch, the Princess was played by his wife, Vera Fokina, and the Koschei by Cecchetti.

Since Diaghilev's death there have been other versions of the ballet, but the story is always told in the same way because this is what Stravinsky's music dictates.

Petrushka

From all over the city of St Petersburg figures muffled against the cold in thick scarves and coats came scurrying through the streets towards the Lent Fair being held on the frozen waters of the River Neva. As they drew nearer, the harsh jangle of the hurdy-gurdies and the throb of fairground machinery sounded louder and louder. Little children jumped up and down with excitement and pelted each other with snowballs.

When at last they arrived, they were overwhelmed by the noise and colour of the fair. The swingboats flew up to the sky and the merry-go-round horses leapt high above the heads of the crowd. Each booth was decorated with striped awning and flags—red and white, blue and yellow—and traders stood by their kiosks crying out their wares and trying to catch the attention of passers-by. People thronged round the stalls and sideshows, jostling each other and stamping their feet on the icy ground in an effort to keep warm. And the old woman selling hot tea from a steaming samovar was doing a busy trade.

The children ran hither and thither, peeping under tent flaps while nursemaids chatted to coachmen and soldiers who were strolling past, looking very dashing in their smart uniforms. Gipsy girls in scarlet petticoats threaded their way through the crowd with trays of ribbons and wooden pegs, plucking at people's sleeves and urging them to buy, or offering to tell their fortunes. An old man shuffled into the square with his barrel organ, and a group of people gathered around him as they recognized the popular songs he was playing. But they were soon distracted by a street dancer who beat a small triangle in time to the music and twirled round and round on her toes with astonishing speed. Then another dancer arrived on the scene and competed with her rival for the crowd's interest by turning somersaults and performing daring acrobatic tricks. The spectators cheered and clapped as they copied each other.

Suddenly everyone looked up at the insistent sound of drums beating. Two drummers were coming to clear a space in front of a large tent for the Showman, who poked his head through the blue curtain, then stepped out from behind the awning. The crowd watched curiously as he took out a flute from the voluminous sleeve of his embroidered caftan. Without saying a word, he began to play a haunting melody. Then all at once he snapped his fingers, and the blue curtains flew open to reveal three figures propped up on metal stands on a little stage. They stared rigidly in front of them—a waxen Ballerina with dainty features and rosy cheeks, a great wooden Moor standing

Ann Jenner as the Street Dancer in The Royal Ballet production.

stiffly erect, clad in turban and gold trousers, and a foolish-looking clown, his rag body limp, his white face drooping sadly on his shoulder.

As soon as the Showman began to play another tune, the motionless puppets started to move with funny little jerks as their limbs were pulled up and down by strings. Faster and faster their feet beat in time to the music until they jumped down from their stands and chased each other round on the frozen ground, falling at last in front of the crowd, which laughed and applauded enthusiastically. It really seemed as if they had come to life, but all too soon the entertainment was over, and the on-lookers were drifting away to other sideshows. At a signal from the Showman the three puppets returned to their places on the stage where they hung quite still once more.

Having packed up his equipment, the old man opened the door of a tiny compartment in his tent and flung the clown inside. Poor Petrushka lay sobbing in a heap on the floor. He was so miserable, a mere puppet, he could not act as he chose, but was condemned to perform just as his master desired. He would be a slave forever.

Below The Showman took out his flute and played a haunting melody. Adrian Grater of The Royal Ballet.

Desperately he beat his head against the walls which imprisoned him and implored the portrait of the Showman, which was the only decoration in his wretched cell, to release him.

'Let me out, let me out—I want to be free!'

Just then the door opened and in stepped the Ballerina, treading delicately on the tips of her toes. Petrushka was overjoyed, for he was deeply in love with her. Indeed, the thought of her was the only thing which made his pathetic life bearable. He jumped up and down with delight and pride, hoping to impress her, but the hard-hearted Ballerina only looked at him in disap-proval, her pretty features of wax set in a fixed expression of disdain. When the clown went so far as to try and embrace her, she turned sharply and strutted out.

Once again, Petrushka was in the depths of despair, and he flung himself about the cell, trying

Below Petrushka implored the portrait of the Showman to set him free. Alexander Grant in The Royal Ballet production.

to find a way of escape, until eventually he broke a hole right through part of the flimsy wooden wall. He picked himself up, and was about to flee to the outside world, when he saw that it led nowhere—he was still captive inside the Showman's tent. Once more he sank to the floor, utterly defeated.

In the compartment next door the scene was very different. There the Moor, in a sumptuously decorated abode, was lying idly on a couch, playing with a coconut. Unlike the clown he was quite content. As he tossed the coconut up in the air, he had only one thought in his wooden head, 'Is it good to eat?' He shook it and banged it on the floor, but he could not open it. Then he drew out his magnificent scimitar and brought it down with a crashing blow, but still the nut would not break. Astonished, he decided that it must be magic. As he knelt down to pray before it, a trumpet

Below The Ballerina danced into the Moor's tent, blowing a gay tune on her bugle. Merle Park of The Royal Ballet.

sounded outside the door, and the Ballerina danced in, blowing a gay tune on her bugle.

Delighted, the Moor forgot all about his coconut, shouted for joy, then grasped the doll around the waist and lumbered round the room with her in a waltz, stumbling and tripping over his own feet in a vain attempt to keep time with the music. Then, tiring of this, he pulled her on to the divan, and sat her on his knee. Although she pretended to be shocked when he tried to embrace her, the Ballerina was secretly enraptured by his attentions and looked most self-satisfied.

All at once there was a crash, the walls of the booth shook, the two sprang apart in guilty surprise, and Petrushka pushed his way in through the door. He had heard the noise, and imagining that the girl he adored had been trapped by his rival, had come to rescue her. With no thought for his own safety, he went up to his gigantic foe and began to rebuke and threaten him. At that the great Moor recovered from his surprise and grunted menacingly with anger. Then he reached for his massive curved sword, and chased the clown round and round the cell,

Below The Ballerina looked at the poor clown disdainfully. Lydia Lopokova and Leonid Massine as they appeared in the United States with the Diaghilev Ballet in 1916.

The Moor pulled the Ballerina on to the divan and sat her on his knee. Merle Park and David Adams.

brandishing it in the air. Just as he was about to catch him, the Ballerina fainted on to the couch, and Petrushka managed to dash out of the door to safety. The Moor was very angry, but not for long. Catching sight of the Ballerina, he picked her up and again sat her on his lap, covering her with clumsy kisses.

Outside the Showman's hut the fair was still in full swing. Although night was falling, everyone was enjoying themselves and had no intention of going home yet. Lanterns had been lit all over the fairground, and peasants were gathering together to sing and dance, swinging each other about with wild abandon. As a group of nursemaids whirled round, the crowd parted, and a great performing bear was led into their midst. It lumbered back and forth and executed a few simple tricks. Some of the children and young ladies were frightened, but it was soon dragged away, and the reckless dancing began again with renewed vigour. The crowd grew more and more excited and rowdy when suddenly there was a commotion from

within the darkened tent of the Showman. There was an immediate hush as cries of anger and pain could be heard, and out rushed Petrushka, chased by the furious Moor waving his treacherous sword, and followed by the Ballerina. All at once the carefree mood of the holiday-makers had vanished and everybody felt strangely uneasy. The Moor gave an angry bellow. There was a flash of polished steel and a terrifying crash as Petrushka's whole body quivered violently and he fell senseless to the ground.

After several minutes of stunned silence a nursemaid rushed to the clown to comfort him. When she saw that he was beyond help, she burst into tears. Someone else ran to fetch a policeman. At this the Showman appeared, laughed and picked up the limp figure of the clown, reminding everyone that he was only a rag doll stuffed with sawdust, that all they had seen had only been part of a play. The people shook their heads in amazement—it had all seemed so real at the time. Then slowly they began to wander off, the nursemaid not convinced and still sobbing. The other stall-holders began to pack up their displays and soon they too had departed.

At last the fairground was dark and quite deserted, save for the Showman, who picked up the rag puppet, and started dragging it across the square as the snow began to fall once more. That instant the old man was startled by an eerie shriek. Peering through the darkness, he saw the ghostly figure of the clown high above the tent, strangely illuminated against the black night sky. Petrushka was free at last, and had come back to haunt his old master in revenge.

Petrushka, as told by Benois and Fokine for the Diaghilev Ballet

The ballet was first produced by Fokine for Diaghilev in Paris on 13 June 1911, the second of the truly Russian ballets. It is about the popular Russian *petrushki,* which are worked partly by gloves and partly by strings and which used to be seen throughout the streets of every town in Russia. Yet the story is one to be found all over the Western world—it tells of the Little Man for whom nothing ever goes right, but who bounces up to try again and again. His English name is Punch, in France he is Pierrot, in Germany Kasper, in Czechoslovakia Kasperlé, and so on. With the help of Fokine, Stravinsky composed his music from folk or popular tunes, as in *The Firebird,* for all the people who come to the fair on the ice. But for the puppets he wrote strange mechanical-sounding tunes which echo their movements, and a wonderfully mysterious music for the Showman as he tells the crowd that his play is ready. Benois, the artist, not only wrote the story, but also designed the scenery and costumes. These showed what you might have seen in the nineteenth century if you had walked up that wide street, the Nevsky Prospekt, to see and hear all the fun of the Lent Fair taking place on the ice.

The first Petrushka was the great dancer Vaslav Nijinsky, in possibly his greatest part. The Ballerina was Tamara Karsavina, and the Moor was Orlov, while Cecchetti played the Showman.

The Prodigal Son

A farmer dwelling in the East seemed to have everything that could be desired. He had worked hard all his life, and as a result had become prosperous, and he had three children – two daughters and a son – of whom he was very proud. He was a kindly man and treated his servants and labourers well. His only concern for his money was to be able to provide for his family so that they should live contentedly together, untroubled by want or strife. His chief delight each day was to return home at sunset with his son to his two daughters, who would be waiting to welcome him, and to pass the rest of the evening in the company of his family.

His daughters often exclaimed at their good fortune in belonging to such a happy household, but his son, who had heard travellers' tales of wonderful cities far away, of feasting and great wealth, grew restless.

'What good will it do me if I spend all my life on this farm?' he grumbled. 'Why, life is short and the world is large! I cannot stay here for ever, where every day I see the same faces, do the same work. I must have adventure before it is too late!'

He sought out his two friends and persuaded them to accompany him on a journey, assuring them that they would soon make their fortunes. Then all three gathered together everything they possessed, packed their bags and prepared to leave.

When they saw what was happening, the sisters were very worried and tried to dissuade their brother from his plan, for they loved him and did not want to see him go. They feared too their father's anger and sorrow when he found out what his son intended. The boy, however, would not listen to their pleas, for he was far too excited, and when his father appeared, would only pause to embrace him briefly. When the old man tried to prevent his son from leaving, the boy, angry and defiant, leapt over the fence surrounding his home, and ran off down the road with his friends

as his sisters wept and his father refused to have anything more to do with him.

After five days and nights the weary travellers arrived at the city they had longed to see. What a strange place it was! The tall buildings and busy streets were magnificent yet frightening. The people were so different from any the boy had known on the farm at home – so many of them, so hostile they seemed. But he was determined to profit from his new freedom in this exciting place, and joined them in their hectic revelry.

Suddenly his attention was caught by a dramatically beautiful woman, the Siren. She paraded around haughtily, draping herself with

The Siren, draped in her brilliant cloak, danced seductively before the crowd. The boy watched amazed, for he had never seen a woman of such exotic charm before. Deanne Bergsma of The Royal Ballet.

Above The boy was captivated by the exotic beauty of the Siren and tried to dance with her, but she entwined herself around him and brought him down exhausted to the ground. Deanne Bergsma and Rudolph Nureyev.

her brilliant magenta cloak and dancing exotically before the assembled throng. The boy was quite enraptured by her seductive charm and tried to caress her and accompany her in her dance. But she, seeing only the heavy gold medallion which he wore around his neck, entwined him with her lithe body and brought him down exhausted to the ground. There the other revellers greedily pounced upon him and quickly stripped him of his clothes, his shoes, and all he possessed. The Siren plucked the medallion from him before running off with her mercenary companions, leaving the poor youth on the ground, almost naked, without shoes or money, and utterly helpless and humiliated.

He lay there for several hours, deserted by his friends and not knowing what to do, until at last he came to his senses. There was no other solution but for him to crawl home to his father and beg his forgiveness. Perhaps at least he would be granted shelter and allowed to stay and work as a servant to the household.

For what seemed like weeks the Prodigal dragged himself back along the road he had come. When at last he could see the roof of his father's farm in the distance, he shed tears of joy. Arriving outside the gate, he collapsed, utterly exhausted. He could go no further.

Just then his two sisters came out of the house and into the garden. Seeing a ragged figure lying on the roadside, they went to his aid, thinking it must be some poor old beggar. To their astonishment, they recognized their long-lost brother. They exclaimed with delight and called out to their father.

As they bent down to help their brother, the old man emerged from the house and seeing his son, immediately opened his arms wide in welcome without uttering a word of admonishment. Very slowly the Prodigal raised himself on to his knees and shuffled forward to his father, who gathered

Below The revellers greedily pounced on the boy to strip him of all his clothes, money and all that he possessed. Rudolph Nureyev as the Prodigal Son in The Royal Ballet production.

73

To their astonishment the sisters realized that the ragged figure was their own brother. Woytek Lowski in the Boston Ballet production.

him up in his arms and carried him into the house, calling the servants to prepare food and drink for celebration and exclaiming joyfully,

'. . . my son was dead, and is alive again; he was lost and is found.'

The Prodigal Son, as told by Balanchine for the Diaghilev Ballet

This biblical story was first produced for the Diaghilev Ballet in Paris on 21 May 1929 by the Russian choreographer Balanchine, who was later to become director of the New York City Ballet. Diaghilev had always wanted to stage a story from the Bible and chose this famous parable. He then invited the young Soviet composer Prokofiev to write the music and the artist Georges Rouault to design the scenery and costumes. Like Balanchine, the choreographer, both composer and artist were deeply interested in biblical history and religious ritual and song, Rouault having just finished his famous set of paintings of Christ in Agony. The collaboration between the three artists, deeply committed to their task, led to the production of a serious and very moving ballet which has stood the test of time ever since. The role of the Prodigal Son was specially written for the young Serge Lifar, who was later to do so much for the Paris Opéra as teacher, leading dancer and choreographer. Other notable dancers in this marvellous role have included Anton Dolin, Rudolph Nureyev, Francisco Moncion, Edward Villella and David Wall, and the ballet is staged by many companies.

Opposite Les Sylphides: a dreamy figure glided amongst her fellow sylphs as if she did not see them, listening attentively for some ghostly call in the distance. Artists of the Festival Ballet in Dame Alicia Markova's production (see page 59).

Les Patineurs
(The Skaters)

It was Christmas Eve, and the air was sharp with the chill of winter. The ground was covered with a thick blanket of snow, and hoarfrost sparkled on the last dead leaves hanging on the blackened branches of the trees. The pond in the middle of the clearing was quite still, its water frozen hard in a solid layer of ice. Night had fallen, but the forest glowed with lanterns of brightly coloured paper which had been suspended from branch to branch.

All at once the peace of this frosty woodland was disturbed by the sound of youthful laughter and shouts in the distance. As the noise grew more distinct, colourful figures could be seen running through the trees. Breathless with excitement and cold, a group of boys and girls clad in brown and blue skating outfits emerged from the forest and stood at the edge of the frozen pool. Then they ventured out on the ice calling to each other.

Opposite Petrushka: (above) Keith Rosson, Jennifer Penney, and Alexander Grant as Petrushka; (below) the ghost of Petrushka appeared (see page 71). Rudolph Nureyev in The Royal Ballet production.

'Is it safe? Will it hold?'
'Yes of course, come on!'

Cautiously at first, to be sure that it would bear their weight, then with more assurance, they slid up and down and spun round, shrieking with delight and proud of their skill. Just then there was a thump and a cry of dismay as one of the boys slipped and fell flat on his back. Everyone laughed at him, but his girlfriend was scornful as she helped him up. Then they all decided to stop for a while and have a snowball fight instead. So they crowded off through the forest, looking for a suitable place for their battle.

No sooner had they gone than two lovers came wandering through the trees. Dressed all in white, they were happy of this opportunity to be alone together. The youth gently set his sweetheart down on the ice, and they clasped hands and set off across the pond, gliding and spinning with

Below The skaters ran through the trees to the frozen pond and ventured on to the ice. Then they spun round and round, shrieking with delight. Dancers of The Royal Ballet.

Suddenly the two girls toppled down on to the ice.
Jeanetta Laurence and Rashna Homji of The Royal Ballet.

effortless grace, tracing wonderful patterns on the frosty surface. They seemed to pay no attention to the steps they made, yet never once did they slip. For a moment they parted hands as the girl twirled round and round, then they came together again and skated off down the frozen stream that led into the pool, leaving the clearing once more deserted.

The noisy group of young people returned to the scene and swarmed over the ice, laughing and whooping at the tops of their voices. The pond grew more crowded as the lovers came back and wove in and out of the other skaters with intricate movements.

Two little girls in scarlet dresses dashed on to the ice, eager to practise and show off their versatility.

'Look at me! Look at what I can do!' they cried to one another. They had not quite mastered the most difficult steps, however, and before long toppled over. But they only giggled the more, scrambled up, and shot off down the stream.

At last came the real experts—a boy and two girls all clothed in blue. They moved with dazzling virtuosity, tearing round the whole pool in a single sweeping arc, spinning dizzily on one spot, and performing daring leaps in the air, yet never even wobbling as they landed.

The snow was beginning to fall afresh as the other skaters made their way back through the trees. The boy in blue hailed them to join him and his companions on the ice, and the whole party slid and turned, laughed and teased each other. At last the snowflakes fell so thick and fast that they all rushed off home to warm their fingers which were numb with cold, leaving the Blue Boy whirling alone in the snow.

Les Patineurs (The Skaters), as performed by The Sadler's Wells Ballet, later The Royal Ballet

This gay scene was first produced by Sir Frederick Ashton at the Sadler's Wells Theatre, London on 16 February 1937. It was designed specially to display the exciting development of English ballet now that the company was truly established in its new theatre. In particular it demonstrated the brilliant dancing of Harold Turner as the Blue Boy. It also marked the first appearance in leading roles of Dame Margot Fonteyn and Sir Robert Helpmann as the two White Dancers, and Michael Somes, whose spectacular leaps as the leader of the *corps de ballet* caught everyone's attention. Meyerbeer's music was arranged by the famous Sadler's Wells conductor Constant Lambert, and the scenery and costumes were designed by one of the dancers, William Chappell, who became a well-known theatrical producer. The ballet is now danced by many companies all over the world.

Cinderella

Cinderella sat in the corner of the kitchen by the hearth gazing into the flames as her stepsisters, busy at the table, quarrelled as usual. They were embroidering a shawl in preparation for the grand ball which was taking place at the King's palace that night, but they could not agree who was going to wear it, and each tried to snatch it away from the other. As the argument grew more heated they tugged harder and harder, until in the end they split the material in two. Frustrated and disappointed, they turned to vent their anger on their poor sister, ordering her to get on with her housework instead of sitting idle by the fire. Then they swept out of the room with their noses in the air.

Picking up her broom Cinderella set to work sweeping the floor, wishing all the time that she too could go to the ball. Sadly she looked down at her ragged dress, which was covered with cinders from the grate. It was the only one she possessed and even if her sisters had given her permission to go, she could never wear that to the palace. Despondently she looked around the room and her eye lighted upon the portrait of her dead mother which hung on the wall and seemed to watch her with tender concern. In despair she considered how her life had changed since her mother had died. Her stepsisters seemed to resent her very presence, so that she spent all her time, when she was not working, hiding in the darkest corner by the fire. She was treated as if she were the humblest scullery-maid. Holding up a lighted candle, she gazed closely at the painting, trying to imagine that her dear mother were still alive. But she could not bear the thought and overcome with grief and despair, she burst into tears.

When her father came down to the kitchen and found his beloved daughter weeping, he was very upset and folding her in his arms tried to comfort her. But he was interrupted by the return of his two formidable stepdaughters and had not the strength to stand up to them. Instead he cowered as they nagged him for spoiling Cinderella and keeping her from her household duties, complaining that he did not consider their comfort at all.

Their grumbling grew louder and louder until they were stamping around the room and shouting at the tops of their voices. All at once a magical tinkling of bells could be heard and a strange shimmering light streamed through the window. Everyone looked up, startled, wondering what this could mean. There on the threshold stood only a pitiful old beggarwoman, dressed in tattered rags and bent over a gnarled stick. Relieved to see nothing more than this pathetic old hag, the Ugly Sisters jeered at her and went to drive her out of the house. But Cinderella, moved by the sight of the old lady whose clothes were even more shabby than her own, stepped forward quietly and offered her a crust of bread. At this the elder of the two sisters screamed aloud.

'Cinderella, you insolent girl! How dare you give this old beggar some of our food! You'll want to take the clothes off our backs next! Just you wait I'll . . .' But suddenly she was struck dumb as the old woman raised her stick high in the air. By the time she had recovered her senses, the old dame had vanished altogether.

There was no time to worry about this odd affair, for the hour had come when the Ugly Sisters must make themselves beautiful with costly cosmetics and extravagant clothes for the royal ball. This was indeed a serious business and required the full attention of the entire household, together with an army of tradesmen—jewelers, dressmakers, shoemakers, hairdressers. The sisters squeezed themselves into corsets so tight that they almost fainted, powdered their faces so thickly that it looked as if they had fallen into the flour bin, and put on such elaborate high curled wigs that they all but toppled over in an effort to keep their balance. When their dresses arrived, the elder sister was so flustered, determined as she was that she alone would be the

Cinderella's father cowered as the Ugly Sisters nagged him. Frederick Ashton, Colin Peasley, Lucette Aldous and Robert Helpmann in the Australian Ballet production.

beauty of the ball, that she struggled into her gown the wrong way round and looked completely ridiculous.

At last they were nearly ready and their dancing-master arrived to give them instruction in the art of graceful movement. His task was not easy, for they were so clumsy and had such big feet that they kept tripping over, or else they found they were pointing in the wrong direction. While the elder executed the dignified steps that she was taught in such a way as to make them seem quite grotesque, her younger sister wrung her hands in despair as she tried in vain to remember the simplest movements of the dance. They quarrelled constantly, of course, competing with each other for the attention of their teacher and each trying to hold his hand. The dancing-master, however, was extremely courteous and patient and continued his lesson until he saw that there

was nothing more that he could teach them. As he politely took his leave, the last items of their gorgeous apparel arrived. Enormous hats were carried in and placed on top of their powdered wigs—their crowning glory indeed. Delighted with themselves, the two spinsters proudly sailed out of the room with all their attendants, sneering as they passed their little sister in her threadbare clothes.

The door slammed shut and Cinderella was left alone. Now all was calm in the kitchen and as she listened she could hear the scuttling of the mice behind the wainscot and the stirring of the glowing coals in the grate. For a while she was lost in her dreams, but then she smiled to herself, remembering the absurd dancing lesson which had just taken place. Jumping up, she seized her broom and pretending that it was her pupil, showed it the steps she had seen the dancing-master try to teach her sisters. Her feet moved so lightly over the floor that her dance was quite unrecognizable from the ungainly attempts of the hefty pair. Laughing aloud, she was thoroughly engrossed in her innocent amusement.

Then, to her surprise, she heard the enchanting music again. When she looked up, she saw the old beggarwoman standing in the corner, and as she stared the walls of the kitchen seemed to disappear. She rubbed her eyes, thinking that she had fallen asleep in front of the cosy fire. But when she opened them again, the old woman had vanished and in her place stood a wonderful creature whose glittering dress encrusted with diamonds so dazzled the poor girl that she drew back timidly. In a voice as clear as crystal the good fairy spoke to her.

'Do not be afraid, dear Cinderella, for I am your

Cinderella laughed to herself as she copied the steps the dancing-master had tried to teach her sisters. Antoinette Sibley of The Royal Ballet.

Fairy Godmother, and I have come to make sure that you *do* go to the ball.'

Cinderella looked at her in astonishment as she waved her wand and the four Fairies of the Seasons flew down, transforming the room into a magical garden before her very eyes. Spellbound, she watched as delicate spring leaves turned from rich green to gold and finally fluttered to the ground before the whole scene was covered in sparkling snow and brilliant stars twinkled in the frosty sky. Gently her godmother took her by the arm and told her to go and fetch a pumpkin. Then she gave a flourish of her magic wand. There was a flash, a puff of smoke and the humble pumpkin was turned into a magnificent carriage fit for a princess, drawn by a team of white mice and driven by coachmen clad in rich livery. It was all so miraculous that Cinderella wondered if she was imagining it after all. She tried to pinch herself awake, but when she looked down at her ragged dress, she found that she was no longer wearing it, but was clothed in the most exquisite gown of white and gold. On her head was a shining crown and round her shoulders was draped a flowing cape of tissue as fine and shimmering as gossamer. Radiantly she turned to thank her godmother, but the good fairy only smiled and gave her one warning.

'Be careful, my child,' she said, 'for you must be sure to return by midnight. At that hour my magic spell will be broken, and your lovely gown will be changed once more to rags.'

The next moment Cinderella mounted the steps of her enchanted coach and was swept off to the ball by her fairy coachmen, surrounded by a host of glistening stars.

The ballroom in the palace glowed with light and all the people assembled there were arrayed in splendid robes of silk and velvet. The Prince had not yet made his appearance, but already the guests were engaged in the intricate formal dances of the court. Their noble dignity was interrupted, however, by the boisterous arrival of the Ugly Sisters, whose preposterous dress and ridiculous behaviour embarrassed everyone. As usual, they soon found a reason for squabbling, to the delight of the royal Jester, who grasped his opportunity to entertain the company by making fun of them.

While the younger spinster looked nervously about her, wishing she had stayed safe at home,

Wayne Sleep of The Royal Ballet as the Jester.

before him and attract his attention, but the Prince did not so much as glance at them and watched instead with polite interest as the musicians played and his courtiers progressed around the floor in their elegant dance.

Suddenly everyone looked up, for one last guest was arriving. Cinderella stood at the top of the grand staircase, her eyes shining with happy excitement. As soon as he caught sight of her, the Prince was transfixed by her loveliness. In wonderment he took her hand and led her down the stairs. They glided across the floor together, Cinderella carrying herself with such grace that all present, even her own sisters, were convinced that she must be the most noble of princesses.

Throughout the evening they danced, never taking their eyes from one another. Overpowered with love for her, the Prince presented her with an orange on a silver tray, for this was the rarest fruit in all his kingdom. Just then he noticed the Ugly Sisters, who were looking thoroughly dejected because he had not once chosen to dance with them. Taking pity he gave them oranges too, but instantly they started to bicker again as the bossy sister snatched the larger fruit from her timorous sister in exchange for the smaller orange which she had been given. No more gallant courtiers invited them to dance and at last there was nothing they could do but partner each other, so they whirled around the ballroom, arm in arm, ignoring the Jester, who perched at the top of the stairs watching and roaring with laughter at their efforts.

As the evening continued, the dancing grew more exhilarating and Cinderella spun round joyfully, oblivious of the time passing and of the fairy's warning. When the Prince drew her to him to kiss her tenderly, her happiness was almost too much to bear. All at once her blissful mood was shattered as she heard the great clock beginning to strike the midnight hour. Horrified, she knew that she must leave without delaying for an instant. But when she tried to slip away, she found that she could not. Wherever she turned the Jester seemed to block her path, and the Prince held her tightly, not wanting to release her for a minute. Frantically she managed to tear herself away just in time. As the twelfth stroke sounded, a little grey figure ran down the stairs, out of the royal palace and off into the cobbled streets. Gone were

and trying to hide to avoid the ordeal of dancing, her domineering sister was anxious that she should at once be granted the most handsome and distinguished of partners. When to her dismay she found that no one asked her to dance but a very short gentleman, she wasted no time in seizing her sister's tall and gallant cavalier and forcing him to partner her instead. As the musicians began to play again, the two girls took their places. Needless to say, their efforts were disastrous, for the younger sister in her fright soon forgot all the steps she had learned, and the elder danced them so clumsily that she had the greatest difficulty in preventing herself from falling flat on her face. Their partners, however, chivalrous to the end, did their utmost to pretend that they did notice these antics.

Eventually, to everyone's great relief, their dance was over, and all the guests stopped to rest for a moment. Then a fanfare of trumpets sounded and the young Prince strode into the hall, escorted by four of his friends. Both sisters tried to bow

Cinderella and the Prince glided across the floor together in perfect harmony. Antoinette Sibley and Anthony Dowell in The Royal Ballet production.

her carriage and coachmen, and her beautiful dress had turned again to rags.

The Prince rushed from the ballroom and stared into the darkness after her. Suddenly he saw one of her golden slippers lying where she had dropped it on the stairs in her haste. Eagerly picking it up, he clasped it to his breast, vowing to seek everywhere until he found the maiden whose tiny foot fitted it, for she had stolen his heart.

At last the Ugly Sisters trudged home from the palace, tired and dispirited. The journey seemed so long, their great feet were swollen and painful and they were almost too tired to move. Worse still, the court Jester would not leave them alone, but persisted in following them and only laughed more heartily when they shouted angrily, telling him to go away.

At home, meanwhile, Cinderella was once more in her place by the hearth, gazing as before into the flames and asking herself if it had all been simply a glorious dream. Sadly she fingered her familiar tattered clothes. Just then she discovered in the pocket of her apron one of the sparkling golden slippers she had worn. She really had been inside the palace, danced at a royal ball and been kissed by the handsome Prince! She would surely dream about this for many weeks to come.

All too soon her rapturous thoughts were interrupted by the noisy return of her stepsisters, who came grumbling into the kitchen, puffing and blowing with fatigue and demanding to be un-dressed and attended to after their exertions. As Cinderella fussed about them, they proudly described all that had happened to them at the ball, elaborating the story, to be sure, so that they appeared to be the heroines of the evening, and boastfully showing her the oranges which the Prince had given them. At this point they were reminded of their recent dispute, and were just about to start another quarrel when a loud fanfare was heard in the street outside. 'Whatever can that be at this late hour?' everyone wondered. To their utter astonishment the door opened, and the Prince himself walked into the kitchen, holding out one golden slipper.

As soon as he had announced his intention to marry the girl whose foot exactly fitted the dainty shoe, the bossy sister pushed herself forward and thrust her foot into the slipper. To her disgust she could only manage to squeeze the tips of her toes inside it, but at least she was comforted by the thought that her sister had no more success in putting on the tiny shoe. Just then Cinderella moved away from the gloomy hearthside. As she did so, the other glittering slipper fell out of her pocket. Seeing this, the Prince was beside himself with excitement and waited impatiently for the Jester to bring a chair for her to seat herself. Then he knelt down in front of the simple girl in her ragged dress and placed both golden shoes on her slender feet. They fitted perfectly. Immediately he embraced her joyfully, and called out to all present that he had found the maiden he sought and that she would be his bride.

The Ugly Sisters were overcome with remorse at the thought of the dreadful way in which they had treated the future Queen of the land. But generous-hearted Cinderella did her best to comfort them, telling them they would always be welcome guests at the palace. The Prince then led her from the kitchen for the last time.

Once more the Fairy Godmother appeared and guided the lovers to the magical garden of the changing seasons and twinkling stars. All the fairies gathered to greet them and bestow their blessings as the Cinderella and her Prince stepped into the enchanted boat awaiting them and sailed away to reign in the land where dreams have no end.

Cinderella, as performed by The Royal Ballet, Covent Garden

Perrault's fairy story has inspired many ballets in the past 150 years. Prokofiev's music was first used by the Soviet choreographer Zakharov at the Bolshoi Theatre, Moscow on 11 November 1945, as a thanksgiving that the War was over. His Cinderella was Galina Ulanova. Since then there have been many versions throughout Russia. The Royal Ballet version was produced by Sir Frederick Ashton at the Royal Opera House, Covent Garden on 23 December 1948. This was Ashton's first attempt at a three-act ballet and the task was made easier because Prokofiev's music was on hand and he could use so many ideas from the traditional and favourite English Christmas pantomime. Also for the very first time he had a large company to fill the stage, for by now the Sadler's Wells dancers were permanently settled at the Opera House. He invited the French artist Jean-Denis Maclès to design scenery and costumes, but in 1965 he re-staged his work with scenery by Henry Bardon and costumes by David Walker. The first Cinderella was Moira Shearer, taking over the role when Margot Fonteyn was injured, with Michael Somes as her Prince. Sir Frederick himself and Sir Robert Helpmann played the Ugly Sisters, Pamela May danced the Fairy Godmother and Alexander Grant was the Jester. Since then many leading dancers have played the role of Cinderella, for it gives them many chances to show the delicacy of their movements and display their ability to play not only the simple kitchen maid but also a Princess at her first ball.

Opposite Giselle: Giselle was lifted on to the farm cart where she was crowned queen of the harvest, and the young people danced joyfully to celebrate the gathering of the crop (see page 23). Elizabeth Anderton in The Royal Ballet production.

Overleaf Cinderella: (left) Anthony Dowell as the Prince and Antoinette Sibley as Cinderella in The Royal Ballet production; (right) Anthony Dowell and Antoinette Sibley with Frederick Ashton and Robert Helpmann as the Ugly Sisters.

Romeo and Juliet

The clock in the market-place had just struck nine when three young men belonging to the Montague household sauntered up the road and into the square. Although his friends Benvolio and Mercutio teased him, Romeo talked of nothing but the Lady Rosaline, with whom he had fallen in love, and he had come out as early as he could in the hope of catching sight of her.

As they waited, the streets gradually filled with people going about their daily work—townsfolk gossiping and shop-keepers calling out their wares, beggars and gipsies trying to attract the attention of passers-by. For a while Romeo allowed himself to be distracted from his romantic daydreams by the mad frolics of three lively gipsy girls, but he soon stopped when a band of youths belonging to the Capulet family and led by the fierce Tybalt swaggered into the square.

Romeo and his friends quickly reached for their swords, for the two families had been sworn enemies for many years and could not pass each other in the street without quarrelling and fighting. Before long the market-place was filled with the sound of clashing steel as both Lord Capulet and Lord Montague arrived on the scene and entered the fray. Soon the square was littered with the bodies of the dead and wounded from the two households.

At last the noise of the skirmish aroused the Prince of Verona himself. He arrived in the thick of the bloodshed and angrily commanded everyone to stop fighting. Then he forced The lords Capulet and Montague to swear a truce with each other, warning them that if ever again their families disturbed the peace of the town, then they themselves would forfeit their lives in punishment. Grudgingly they laid down their

Opposite The lovers embraced each other in despair, unable to bear the thought that Romeo must leave. Patricia Ruanne as Juliet and Rudolph Nureyev as Romeo in the Festival Ballet production.

weapons at the feet of the slain men and went on their way in silence. They had made their promise to the Prince, but there was still vengeance in their hearts.

That same day, in a quiet part of the city far removed from the bustle of the market-place, a girl was playing with her doll, quite unaware of the angry scene which had taken place that morning. She was a pretty child with long hair and

Romeo and his two friends, Benvolio and Mercutio sauntered into the market-place. David Ashmole, David Wall and Michael Coleman of The Royal Ballet.

a very lively manner, and she broke into peals of laughter as she teased her Nurse, running round and round her until the old lady was quite dizzy.

It seemed as if she had not a care in the world, but even as she was engrossed in her game, the door opened and her father and mother, the Lord and Lady Capulet, ushered in a youth whom they introduced as the noble Paris, a kinsman of the Prince himself. The time had come, they had decided, that their daughter should take a husband. Who could be better than this handsome and thoroughly suitable young man? He in his turn was enchanted by the girl, but Juliet was too innocent to understand the meaning of his gallant attentions, and as soon as he and her parents had left the room she resumed her game.

The Nurse, however, saw that she must gently dissuade her charge from such childish activities, for as she told Juliet, she was fast growing up and becoming a woman, and must behave with according dignity. It was the first time that Juliet had ever considered herself in such a way, and she felt strangely apprehensive as she contemplated the new role she must adopt.

That evening there was great excitement in the Capulet household, for preparations were being made for a grand masked ball. Lights shone from every window of the palace as the first important guests began to arrive at the gates.

Loitering by the wall were the three Montague youths, ever hopeful of a glimpse of Lady Rosaline. At last she arrived, but she haughtily passed by the three boys, pausing only to toss Romeo a rose from her bouquet, before she swept into the palace on the arm of Tybalt. Clutching the treasured flower, Romeo determined to follow her and join the festivities, despite the fearful risk of being found in Capulet territory. The three intrepid friends put on masks and cloaks and strode in through the gates and up to the great house, thrilled with the sense of adventure and danger.

When they entered the magnificent ballroom, the guests were proceeding with dignified steps in a stately dance. As soon as it had finished, the doors opened and Juliet stood hesitantly on the threshold. Her flowing locks had been braided around her head, and her childish dress had been discarded for a beautiful robe of white and gold. She was no longer a little girl, but a lovely maiden,

When Juliet appeared, all the guests gazed at her in admiration, for she was no longer a little girl but a lovely maiden. Marilyn Rowe in the Australian Ballet production.

and when she shyly took her place among the dancers next to Paris, it was clear that all the other guests were watching her in admiration.

A new dance began, and as Juliet moved round with Paris, Romeo, who had been engrossed in his pursuit of Rosaline, looked up and saw her for the first time. Their eyes met, and they seemed to gaze at each other for an eternity. At last the music stopped and Juliet broke away from her partner to take up her lute and play with her friends to entertain the assembled guests. Nevertheless, she could not stop herself from stealing glances at the stranger, and he, all thoughts of Rosaline forgotten, broke into the group of girls to reach Juliet in their midst.

Immediately Romeo's friends saw the danger of this meeting, and did everything they could to distract the other guests. Once again Paris took Juliet's hand, but Romeo intervened to dance with her alone. At this point Tybalt organized another courtly measure for the whole company, and the young couple were forced to separate and join the general movement, only passing each other momentarily as they progressed across the room. Finally Juliet, quite bewildered by what had happened, made the excuse that she was feeling faint, and left the ballroom as the other dancers also retired to take their seats in the banqueting hall.

Soon the ballroom was deserted, and as the candles burned low, Juliet crept back stealthily. She was confused and troubled by this unexpected meeting with the masked stranger who had seemed to exercise an awesome power over her, so that she was aware of no one else in the room but this man. She was not long lost in contemplation, however, for she was interrupted by the return of the mysterious dancer himself.

When she begged him to tell her who he was, Romeo cast aside his mask. Then he disclosed his identity and at the same time declared his ardent love for her. Juliet, mindless of the danger, could only yield to the force which drew her towards Romeo. Suddenly the lovers were interrupted by Tybalt, who had seen the youth unmasking himself and recognized him. He immediately grasped his sword, ready to fight.

Fortunately just at that moment the other guests began to return to the ballroom. Mercutio and Benvolio, joking and teasing, did their best to appease the hostile Tybalt and divert his attention. Soon Lord Capulet himself bade Romeo welcome, for he was heedful of the Prince's warning and was determined that neither fighting nor bitter feeling should spoil this night of happy festivity. However, Mercutio and Benvolio had tasted enough danger for one evening, and persuaded Romeo that it was time to depart before anything more serious should occur. So glancing back once more at Juliet, Romeo took up his cloak and followed them out of the palace.

The party was finished at last. The lights had been extinguished in the great reception halls and the house was dark and quiet; but Juliet was too excited to sleep. The night was warm, so pausing only to cover her shoulders with a thin shawl, she pushed open the shutters of her room and went out on to the balcony. The garden below her was bathed in soft moonlight, and as she gazed up at the stars and thought of all that had happened that evening, she fancied she heard a slight sound. Looking down, she saw the shadowy form of a man emerge from the trees. The figure stood at the

foot of the staircase leading up to the balcony. It was Romeo.

Without hesitating, she rushed down the stairs and into his arms. Ecstatically they embraced each other, and pledged vows of undying love.

The next day found Romeo again in the market-place. This time he took no notice of what was going on around him, paid no attention to the merry wedding-procession that was winding its way along the road, nor even to his friends Mercutio and Benvolio and the three gipsy girls who had amused him the day before. Instead, he was entirely absorbed by the thought of Juliet and of when he might contrive to see her again. At length he was roused by the sight of the Nurse, who came puffing into the square, holding up a letter from Juliet. While she recovered her breath, the boys teased her and tried to steal the precious note, but at last Romeo held it in his hand. He tore it open, and was overjoyed to read that Juliet would be awaiting him that afternoon at the cell of a priest, Friar Laurence, where they would be married in secret.

A few hours later, in the gloomy chamber where the priest lived, Romeo waited. He had not been there many minutes before Juliet, accompanied by her Nurse, came down the steps and into the cell. The poor old Nurse was weeping at the idea of such an ill-advised union, but the two lovers were too happy to allow their joy to be spoilt, and within a short while and with simple solemnity, the priest had joined their hands in Holy Matrimony.

The ceremony over, Juliet returned home for the time being with her Nurse, while Romeo emerged into the bright sunlight and made his way once more to the market-place, which was still bustling with the noisy celebration of the wedding-party. Today nothing could disturb his calm, happy mood, and when Tybalt arrived, brandishing his sword, he refused to fight. He believed that his marriage to Juliet, as yet secret, would later be the means to end the age-old enmity between the Montagues and Capulets.

Mercutio, shocked by what he believed to be his friend's cowardice, could no longer bear the taunts of the enemy, took up his sword and rushed into the fray, despite Romeo's efforts to prevent him. The fighting was bitter, and to everyone's horror, Tybalt succeeded in stabbing

At last Romeo held the precious note in his hand. Kelvin Coe as Romeo and Edna Edgley as the Nurse in the Australian Ballet production.

Mercutio in the back. Mercutio bravely tried to make little of his wound, joking and chattering in his usual manner, but the sword-thrust had been fatal. Suddenly he collapsed, dying and cursing the houses of both Montague and Capulet with his final breath.

At the sight of the pitiful corpse of his best friend, Romeo was at last roused to anger. Beside himself with grief and fury, he seized Mercutio's sword and flew at Tybalt, killing him after a brief and cruel struggle. Too late he realized what an atrocity he had committed, and when Lady Capulet, alarmed by the uproar, arrived to see the body of her favourite nephew lying covered with blood on the ground, he was quickly led away from the scene by Benvolio, who was fearful of the consequences of such a dreadful deed. The feud had been resumed in all its violence.

The next morning the rising sun shone through the shutters in Juliet's bedroom revealing the two lovers clasped in each other's arms on the great bed. Romeo stirred, and waking, gently tried to disengage himself from Juliet's embrace and to steal out of the room through the window without disturbing her. But she awoke and tried to persuade him not to leave her so soon. Again they clung to each other passionately, but knew that he must depart at once for fear of being caught in the house of his sworn enemies.

Just in time he jumped down to the garden from the window, for Lord and Lady Capulet entered Juliet's room with Paris to tell her that there would be no further delay, that she must resign herself to becoming the wife of Paris. When Juliet refused and implored her father to be merciful, he angrily pushed her aside, and warned her that he would accept no more excuses, that she must prepare herself to be married immediately. Then he left the room in a temper, accompanied by his wife and Paris, leaving his daughter alone in utter despair.

She dared not tell her parents of her marriage after Romeo had killed their beloved nephew, yet nor could she betray her vows and allow herself to be wed to Paris. What could she possibly do? At last she remembered the one person who might be able to help her. Hastily covering herself with her shawl, she ran as fast as she could in the direction of Friar Laurence's cell.

When she had poured out her woes to the priest, she waited anxiously, as he paced the room in silence and considered the matter in deep thought for some time. At last he revealed his plan

Mercutio took up his sword and rushed to attack Tybalt. Desmond Doyle as Tybalt and Michael Coleman as Mercutio.

to her. Handing her a tiny glass bottle, he told her that it contained a drug so powerful that it induced a sleep like death. She must wait until she was alone and then take the potion, which would immediately send her to sleep. When her family came to wake her, everyone would think that she had died, and would take her body to the Capulet tomb. The priest meanwhile, would have sent word of the stratagem to Romeo, who would arrive in time to rescue her when she awoke.

On returning to her room, Juliet hid the glass phial under her pillow. After her parents had come once more to speak with her, she finally agreed to marry Paris, showing neither joy nor sorrow at the prospect, for she knew her promise meant nothing, and all the while was thinking of the dreadful task which awaited her.

Alone once more, she took out the small glass phial and stared at it, wondering at the terrible power of the substance it contained. Trembling with apprehension, for she was terrified at the thought that she might find herself buried alive, she quickly swallowed the bitter liquid.

The drug acted so swiftly, numbing the blood in her veins, that she had hardly time to drag herself to the bed before her strength failed her and she fell, her face deathly pale, her limbs cold and her body limp—to all appearances quite dead.

A few minutes later the door of the room was pushed open, and a group of Juliet's young friends entered. They carried garlands of flowers to prepare her for her wedding. Puzzled that she should remain asleep so late on the morning of such an exciting day, they went up to the bed and tried to rouse her. But when they saw her pallid face and touched her icy fingers, they cried out in horror. Just then, the Nurse came in carrying the wedding-dress. At the sight of the weeping girls she rushed to the bedside, and seeing the lifeless body, immediately broke into piteous sobs. Alarmed by the noise, Juliet's parents came

quickly to the room. They too were overcome with sorrow at this new tragedy following so soon after the death of their kinsman Tybalt.

Inside the vaulted tomb of the Capulet family it was dark and gloomy. The feeble candlelight flickered against the moss-covered walls, as the funeral procession moved slowly past the body of Juliet which had been placed on top of the coffin in which she was to be laid to rest. The friends and relatives of the girl, clad in black mourning-dress, bowed their heads in sorrow, while the hooded monks solemnly intoned the Last Rites of the Dead. When the mourners had paid their final respects to the body, they passed out of the vault. Only Paris lingered behind to take one last look at the beautiful girl who was to have been his bride.

All this while Romeo had been hiding in the shadows. Unable to bear the sight of Paris touching his own Juliet, he rushed out and flung him aside, striking him dead with one blow of his dagger. Then he snatched up the body of his sweetheart, quite distraught with grief, for he had

Above Juliet implored her parents not to force her to wed Paris. Lynn Seymour and Derek Rencher of The Royal Ballet.

Below The two lovers clung to each other passionately but knew that Romeo must leave without delay. Marilyn Rowe and Kelvin Coe of the Australian Ballet.

heard nothing of Friar Laurence's plan, and had believed like everyone else that she was truly dead. Without her his life was empty, unendurable. Holding Juliet's hand and gazing at her face, he took a phial of poison from his belt and drank its venomous contents. Within seconds he had fallen dead at her feet.

A faint colour infused the ashen cheeks of the lifeless girl. Very gradually the tips of her fingers moved. Her eyelids fluttered and her body stirred. Juliet was awaking from her sleep of death. She opened her eyes and stared in fright at the grim walls around her. Where was she? Then she remembered the plan, but even as she prepared to wait for Romeo to come and rescue her, she saw the two bodies on the ground beside her. One was Paris, and the other was her Romeo. Aghast at the thought of her lover gone, unable to contemplate a life without him, she seized his blood-stained dagger. Plunging it deep into her heart, she reached out as she died to hold him in one last embrace.

Romeo, quite distraught with grief, snatched up the body of his beloved Juliet. Lesley Collier and Wayne Eagling in The Royal Ballet production.

Romeo and Juliet, as told by Kenneth MacMillan for The Royal Ballet, Covent Garden

The first attempt to create a ballet from Shakespeare's tragedy was made in St Petersburg by the Russian ballet-master Valberg as long ago as 1809. There have since been many versions of the tale danced in Russia, so it is not surprising that the Russian composer Prokofiev was commissioned to write a score for the Kirov Theatre. But when it was ready in 1938, the director rejected it as being far too modern. So it was not until the Kirov ballet visited Moscow on 11 January 1940 that the Soviet choreographer Leonid Lavrovsky produced his famous version at the Bolshoi Theatre, Moscow. This was an overwhelming success, not only because of the exquisite dancing of his Juliet and Romeo, Galina Ulanova and Konstantin Sergeyev, and the exciting portrayal of Mercutio by Koren, but also because of the dancing and acting of the rest of the cast and the scenery and costumes by the artist Peter Williams.

Since that time there have been many versions, which have been more or less successful. Most of them stay close to Shakespeare's plot, for Prokofiev composed his music with the help of a famous Russian theatrical director, Radlov, who insisted that the story must follow that of the play. The Lavrovsky ballet is still danced in Leningrad, and Sir Frederick Ashton created a beautiful version for the Royal Danish Ballet in 1955. But Kenneth MacMillan's version has seldom been absent from The Royal Ballet's repertoire since it was first staged on 9 February 1965 with scenery and costumes by Nicholas Georgiadis. His Romeo and Juliet were Christopher Gable, now an actor, and Lynn Seymour, with David Blair giving a memorable performance as Mercutio. Since then the leading roles have been danced by all the soloists of The Royal Ballet, each of whom has made their own contribution to Shakespeare's tragic tale of love.

Acknowledgments

The author and publisher would like to thank the ballet companies and individuals listed below for permission to reproduce photographs in this book.

American Ballet Theatre
photo: Costas 54
photo: Kenn Duncan 27
photo: Louis Péres 19
photo: Martha Swope 21, 42 *top*

The Australian Ballet 22, 31, 33 *bottom*, 80
photo: David Parker 13, 90, 92, 94 *bottom*

Boston Ballet
photo: Bela Kalman 50, 74

The Festival Ballet
photo: Anthony Crickmay 44, **45**
photo: Reg Wilson **75, 88**

Houston Rogers 65 *bottom*

Nesta Macdonald 61, 69 *right*

Mansell Collection 63

National Ballet of Canada
photo: Anthony Crickmay 24
photo: Andrew Oxenham 8, 11 *top*, 38, 55 *top*
photo: Martha Swope 16, **35**

The Royal Ballet, Covent Garden 11 *bottom*, 65 *top*
photo: Anthony Crickmay 2, 24, 32, 33 *top,* 37, 40, 53 *bottom,* 59, 62, 64, 68 *right*, 72, 73 *top*, 77, 78, 82, 83, 93, 94 *top*, 95
photo: Alan Cunliffe 29, 73 *bottom*
photo: Frederika Davis 15
photo: Zoe Dominic 60
photo: Houston Rogers 30
photo: S. Hurok 53 *top*
photo: Nigel Luckhurst 42 *bottom,* 49
photo: Donald Southern 55 *bottom*
photo: Leslie E. Spatt 6, 9, 10, 43, 52, 67, 68 *left*, 69 *left*, 70, 81, 89
photo: Reg Wilson **17, 36, 46–7, 57, 58, 76, 85, 86–7**

The Royal Ballet School
photo: Reg Wilson **48**

The Royal Danish Ballet
photo: Reg Wilson **18**

Figures in **bold** type refer to colour illustrations.